BECOMING

Unforgettable

Uncovering the Essence of the Woman

EBUN AKPOVETA

authorHOUSE®

AuthorHouse™
1663 Liberty Drive
Bloomington, IN 47403
www.authorhouse.com
Phone: 1-800-839-8640

Published by AuthorHouse   09/17/2012

ISBN: 978-1-4772-2626-1 (sc)
ISBN: 978-1-4772-2625-4 (e)

Dedication

To everyone I have met along the way in this walk. Everyone who has contributed to my life experience, increased my knowledge and enhanced my quality of life.
To every relationship, encounter and contact that has allowed me to experience the full essence of being a woman. Thank you for the gift of your time, friendship, support and encouragement.

To all the women in my life, past present and future, my sisters, friends, mother, Aunties, colleagues, daughters, clients and those I am yet to meet.
Thank you for allowing me to be me.

To every searching woman, may you find the true value and power of being a woman, walk as your true self and experience the dignity of being a woman.

Contents

Introduction

Women all over the world are caught up in different stages of the same struggle. Some women face it in public life and for others it's in their homes or both places. In spite of the increasing number of women who have become qualified professionals in various sectors, many are still struggling for the right to have an education. While some women enjoy the benefits of freedom of speech and equal rights, some have to keep silent until they are directly spoken to and permitted to speak. While some are campaigning for equal pay for equal work irrespective of gender, many are still struggling with the right to work outside the home. Various extremes experienced by women. Nonetheless, whatever stage you are as a woman, undoubtedly, one factor that can greatly impact on the quality of life of any woman is the personal qualities she exhibits.

The question today is how can we effect change or are women stuck with the qualities that are not serving them. Are some women born with qualities that make them confident, unforgettable, high achievers or do they acquire and develop qualities through which they become unforgettable? Are some other women born subservient followers or do they learn to become that way? In other words, is subservience a trait or is it learned. In the born or made debate, the general consensus is that though we cannot chose how we are born, we can chose how and what we allow make us. Various studies also show that leaders are one third born and two third made yet that information is like a well-kept secret! Its implication is that people can develop the qualities they desire and the absence of such desirable qualities does not equate the lack of ability but rather it reflects it's under development.

There has not been a greater need for that answer now than there has been before with the increasing frustration experienced by women as they grapple with their identity. Today's women find themselves in a quandary and are hugely challenged by a society bent on dictating to them what to do, how to be and how to feel without fully understanding her.

Women have for centuries been led by a male dominated society which has contained and prevented many women from fully exploring and experiencing their full potentials and strength. They have tried to make her into what I describe as the living dead! Where alive she is to stay boxed up, silent, emotionless, and still. Yet inside her, the woman knows something about that position doesn't feel right. Unfortunately many women stay contained within the set parameters but ever so often, the box gets too small and some women get the urge to explore life. The challenge of integrating these two positions, the conflict between the internal and the external has presented modern women with a great dilemma of how to be women further fuelling their stress.

It is amazing that the only commonality between races, religions, sects, traditions, cultures, theologians and even politicians is the continuous perpetuation of the subordination of women. They are frequently categorised as the weaker sex, assigned gender based roles, they experience glass ceiling in employment and earn about 25 per cent less than men in the same role. This has been happening for centuries both overtly and covertly even in places where you would least expect it. This has led many women into an inferiority positioning where women are at the bottom of the hierarchy just because of their gender. Martin Luther King encapsulated the basis for equality when he said "I look to a day when people will not be judged by the colour of their skin, but by the content of their character." Every dark skinned person out there agrees with this but where do women stand. Should women continue to be judged, classed, paid, positioned and treated on the basis of her gender or on the basis of her ability or can women hope that truly what is good for the goose is good for the gander? The difficulties with addressing such issues is that the male folks are the beneficiaries and as such do not have a vested interest in the topic while the females who do are blacklisted and labelled trouble makers and feminist.

The extent of the problem can be seen in the natural benefit attached to being male and the automatic disadvantage of being female. If we consider that two people of the same age with the same qualification and skills are told that one can be whatever he wants to be and the other is not expected to have an opinion neither are her opinions listened to or even sought all because one is male and the other is female. Such levels of discrepancy in treatment illustrate the scale to which women's potential are being limited and their abilities undermined. In some African communities, at the announcement of the birth of female children the older people jokingly say a prostitute has been born. Though they don't use that particular word, they say it in their local dialect or vernacular to make it sound normal and as a joke but in actual fact it is insulting and it undermines the value of the newly born defenseless child. When on the other hand a male child is born the announcement is heralded with much jubilation and back slapping celebrating the powers of the father. As astounding as it may seem, women cannot drive a car in public alone in some Arab countries and up until 2005 women in some countries were not allowed to decide who ruled them because they had no voting rights. Women have had to contend for every inch of what they have and so women's issues are laced with words like women were *"allowed"* implying resistance and opposition.

When a woman with two perfectly working eyes cries and laments that she only has one eye when she has seven beautiful, healthy children just because six of them are female and only one of them is male then one might begin to understand the impact of societies expectations and the burden it places on women. Where instead of being happy for the birth of their children they are in a panic that their partner will leave them just because they don't have any male children who will be heirs and maintain the family name. There is a great importance and urgency at this time in history to start giving equal value to the female person. Perhaps a cue in the right direction taken by the British Monarchy is worthy of emulation with the recent amendment in the succession rights. Where from now a first born child succeeds in the throne irrespective of their gender thereby abolishing the age old tradition where a first born child who is female is bypassed in favour of a younger male child. A welcome into the world which programs females for a second class and substandard existence, actions which present girls with an image of insignificance and that they are not counted as children.

When the purpose of a thing is unknown, abuse they say is inevitable

Many women of African descent are faced with this challenge and even those in the diaspora are not excluded.

When the purpose of a thing is unknown, abuse as the saying goes is inevitable. So the society, it's leaders, politicians, everyone needs to begin to see the true value of the woman and help her overcome years of exploitation. We need to help our women folk develop their innate qualities which has been suppressed so that we can truly address the issues of maltreatment and displacement of women which is prevalent in today's society.

In some places women have no rights, no voice and definitely no choice when it comes to who and when she shares her body. Some children as young as thirteen years old are given to eighty years old men to bed them as child bride. This is again a form of legalized rape, child abuse and torture! The sad truth is that all these scenarios are still happening in some homes, communities and countries. Even the developed countries as they pride themselves still have some of such subjection of women and daughters behind closed doors the one place where they should feel safe.

There is no animal farm. You know the allegorical story by George Orwell where some animals claimed all animals are equal but some are more equal than the others? It is not true! No matter how much they try to weld the rope, everyone is equal, male-female, black-white, every one of all colour, race and creed. The continued normalization of the oppression of women is forcing many women to take a stance of hardness to protect and prove themselves leaving the society bereft of the femininity of the woman, a core part of female attributes.

Years ago they kept women in this *living dead box* by keeping education, employment, social interactions, voting rights amongst other building blocks out of her reach thereby limiting her circle of influence. This hitherto accepted positioning of women is keenly contested today mainly because of a higher level of education and exposure being experienced by women. Ideologies are being questioned, rationales challenged and male led theological interpretation

__Women blossom when they are esteemed and valued__

and exegesis are being contested. In as much as women celebrate and value the changes they have witnessed so far, it is still very eagerly resisted especially by the male folks as women gain more grounds and are getting repositioned in society.

Some of the male gender have championed and welcomed these changes but like everything in life there is still major opposition especially behind closed doors and in the nuclear family relations. Many males have felt more threatened, have had to deal with loss of power while some have resorted to using more force to maintain control. There is genuine confusion being experienced by some males who in principle agree with the equal treatment of women but in the practicality of their day to day life find it difficult to implement. This plays out in their reluctance to relinquish the automatically assumed male privileges in relationships, top level management, politics and even ministry. Its effect is seen on various levels of society where in individuals it breeds anger, hatred and depression and in society it has led to a protracted struggle between males and females resulting in more and more people being disillusioned about the institution of marriage, increased divorce and single parenting. Good judgment tells us that if a thing is getting worse something needs to change. Albert Einstein is famously quoted as saying the definition of insanity is doing the same thing over and over expecting a different result. There is no denying that the relationship between men and women is getting worse and the divorce rate is getting higher in every society, culture and religion.

Various attempts have been made by governments at national and European level where special funds and programmes have been put in place to support and address the plight of women. Yet with each passing year more and more women are being abused, killed, raped and deprived of their basic human needs. Women themselves in their desire to become unforgettable have mistaken it for beauty. They end up spending so much time and money on layers of face powder, designer lipstick and clothes until they find it's not enough as they are quickly replaced with a younger more beautiful model. Some think it's the size of their bust and they are willing to go through all kinds of treatments that can make even the flat chested into a busty mama! They have unwittingly funded many silicone implant companies and turned their founders into millionaires. Some others think it's in the length or smoothness of their legs and have endured hours of painful waxing while others place more emphasis on having a silky sing song voice or lengthened and false lashes. Sadly, it has proved not enough as even women possessing all these physical assets have been abandoned for the next rave of the moment. Looking good they say is good business. However, unless you want to make a living as a model or a kept woman then you might need more attributes.

Memorable, remarkable, impressive, extraordinary, haunting, treasured, etched in the mind of others is the one desire of many women. Sadly, the one thing many women desire and crave is the very thing societies all over the world conspire to deny her—*the need to be esteemed and valued,*. Some women want their manager's approval and others it's their family, kids or the small group they belong to. Many women are wondering if people will ever take their ideas seriously. Will they ever make a mark or have someone esteem them to the point they say "You are unforgettable." Some women wonder if they will ever go from ordinary to exceptional or if it is reserved for only a select few with special opportunities. The truth is that no matter where you are in your life right now if you put your heart to it then you can. It might be hard—in fact it will be hard, even rocky but every woman can do it including you.

Unforgettable is a describing feature that suggests a positive attribute of an action, person or a thing and it usually brings a good feeling. It sneaks up on you when you have your mind on something or someone else bringing a smile to you. Though not all women will be world or nation changers, yet each woman can affect her home, her children, her community and her school amongst others. The lives of great achievers have been impacted by women for generations where for some; it's their mother, sisters or even their wives or grandmothers who are unforgettable in their lives.

Although women of all colour, size, shape and ethnicity have been faced with various levels of limitations nonetheless every once in a while we see that dashing star that makes a mark and dares to be different. We see that woman who steps out of the box and decides not to allow anything stop her. No matter where you've come from, what you have come through, no matter what you have or don't have, today that woman can be you.

Becoming Unforgettable is the insightful analysis of the life an ordinary woman who by one singular act became unforgettable. It extracts and highlights twelve qualities of an Unforgettable woman and the underpinning principles. This time tested principles are capable of breaking barriers and transforming the life of every woman who is ready for her change. Though we credit the slogan, "yes we can" to Barrack Obama, the first black American president winners have for centuries held that same belief—*yes I can*. I wish that every woman out there reading this book will lift up her hand and make a little fist waving that hand in the air as you mouth the words "yes I can." I don't know what you have been told can't be done. I don't know who has told you that you can't. Maybe a significant other in your life has told you that you cannot make it without them. Maybe this person is your father, mother, school teacher, boyfriend or even your spouse.

The hope is that at the end of reading *Becoming Unforgettable*, you will be inspired to yearn for, acquire and adapt principles that will unlock the gifts, talents and abilities within you. That *Becoming Unforgettable* will help you develop qualities through which you can break and walk free of every imposed box and limitation in your life. People have excelled and now it is your time to shine, it is your turn to increase. Your unforgettable moments begin right now.

Ebun Akpoveta

PART ONE

Women's Stories

One

A line-up of Unforgettable women— the Female World Changers

History records many high achievers who because of or in-spite of their limitations pushed the boundaries and challenged the status quo. It documents how for century's women's lives have been plagued with struggles that are beyond race, age, beauty, education and wealth. Yet from there arose women who were not vying for position or self-gratification nor were they trying to change the world. Rather, they were women who chose to stand for something. The choice women face today is to either let people, traditions, culture, policy, fear, the recession and even religion stop you because you are women or you can dare to be different.

If you don't stand for something, you will fall for anything.

Looking back, women appear to be living in better times today than those who lived decades ago and were still able to transform their world. As *Becoming Unforgettable* encourage and challenge women to be the best they can possibly be, it is vital that women work together and not in competition with each other, if not they again miss the point and destroy purpose. There is enough for every woman who dares to be different. There is enough for every woman who reaches for excellence as over the years a few ordinary women just like you and I have dared to make a change.

As far back as the 1800's when there were no phones, family support groups or welfare officer's women like Susan B. Anthony (1820-1906), together with Elizabeth Cady Stanton, fought for women's right to vote. Civil rights movement cannot forget a woman like Rosa Parks (1913-2005) who made history when she refused to give up her seat to a white person on a crowded bus. Though it is reported that she was not the first person to resist bus segregation she however had her case go all the way to court and it became a cornerstone of the civil rights movement.

Dolores Huerta fought for the right to a minimum wage, unemployment insurance, paid holidays, and retirement benefits for farm workers. Joan of Arc (1412-1431) in the 1400's was a national hero who led the resistance to the English invasion of France in the Hundred Years War. Look at that! Though she was only 19 years old when she was wrongly accused of heresy and burnt at the stakes, twenty-five years after her execution, an inquisitorial court pronounced her innocent, and declared her a martyr. In more recent times, women like Mother Theresa (1910-1997) devoted her life to aiding the sick and poor people throughout the world. She was originally from Albania yet she didn't allow the fact that she was a migrant limit her. She had to learn English in Ireland and she also had to learn Bengali language in India to be able to communicate and teach.

History records women like Eleanor Roosevelt (1884-1962) a champion of human rights who strove to further the cause of women, black people, the poor and the unemployed. She was the first lady of the United States from 1933-1945 but she didn't just hang around looking pretty. She actively supported policies and became an advocate for civil rights. Even after tragedy befell her and she was widowed, she didn't wallow in self-pity but went on to be an international author, speaker, politician, and activist. She worked to enhance the status of working women and supported the formation of the United Nations amongst other things.

Mary McAleese served as the eighth President of Ireland from 1997 to 2011. She was the world's first woman to succeed another as president. She was re-elected unopposed for a second term in office in 2004. She addressed issues concerning justice, social equality, social inclusion, anti-sectarianism and reconciliation. She also made brave attempts to reach out to the unionist community in Northern Ireland

and she was ranked the 64th most powerful woman in the world by Forbes.

Dr. Mary Elizabeth Carnegie (1916-2008) was an educator and author in the field of nursing who established the first nursing program for blacks. In 1945, she became the first dean of the School of Nursing at Florida A. & M. University and she was known for breaking down racial barriers and preserving the history of African American nurses. At a time when black nurses at some hospitals were not allowed to identify themselves as "Miss," only "Nurse," Dr. Carnegie insisted on the proper honorific. She broke the colour barrier as the first black nurse appointed to the board of the Florida Nurses Association. Though her spot on the board was a more "be seen and not heard from" position, her drive and determined to put a dent in the racial inequality in the nursing field motivated her to speak in their meetings making sure she voiced her opinions this eventually led to her being granted her full rights and responsibilities within the FSNA.

It is easier to blame ones backgrounds and misfortunes. It is even understandable how easily that can happen. In the line-up of unforgettable women we have been through they didn't have it easy yet they made it possible for women all over the world to have a voice today. You too can add your quota, you can make a difference because this time it is your move. You might feel stuck and think it is too late for you to make a change. For anything you want badly enough it can never be too late. Even if it can't be done for this generation, it will be great to leave a legacy for the next generation of women. These female forerunners in their own way and professional capacities paved the way for many including the poor, women, farmers, nurses and people of colour. They negotiated rights to vote, to work, to equal pay and even to life! There are pockets of opportunities available today to create a better future for our daughters and ultimately better homes for our sons. If I can borrow the mission of Web of Hearts Foundation we can ensure "happy women, happy society."

If you want something badly enough then it is never too late to try

Being a Woman is Not a Limitation

Where do you stand, among the makers or wonderers? In motivational circles, they say "There are two types of people in the world, those who make things happen and those who wonder what happened." Following others can seem safe and less challenging, however some more women have to stand up like these ordinary women who accomplished extraordinary feats. You too can do something today. Trail blazers like Clara Barton (1821-1912) was the founder and first president of the American Red Cross, Grace Hopper (1906-1992) invented one of the first easy-to-use computer languages, Shirley Chisholm (1924-2005) was the first black woman to serve in the House of Representatives in 1968 while Bessie Coleman (1893-1926) was the first African American to become a licensed airline pilot and the first American of any race or gender to hold an international pilot license. We see women of every colour and age, who made it into the lineup of unforgettable women.

Two types of people in the world, those who make things happen and those who wonder what happened

We have Dr. Mae C. Jemison who became the first black woman in space aboard SPACELAB J on Mission STS-47 and Amelia Earhart (1897-1937) the first woman to fly across the Atlantic Ocean. Ellen Ochoa was the first Hispanic woman to be named an astronaut and Dr. Sally Ride was the youngest American astronaut ever to orbit Earth.

Closer to home we have Margaret Thatcher the first woman in European history to be elected prime minister and also the first British prime minister to win three consecutive terms in the 20th century. Victoria Woodhull (1838-1927) was the first woman to be nominated for the U.S. presidency and Elizabeth Blackwell (1821-1910) was the first American woman awarded a medical degree by a college after she was rejected by all the major medical schools in the nation because of her gender. We can easily see that rejection is not a new thing! So it should not limit you. Try, try and try again. Try something different.

History could not ignore some women as they were given Nobel prizes for their accomplishments and today you too can rewrite your story, don't let gender determine how far you can go, what you can or cannot do, who you can or cannot be. Marie Curie (1867-1934) was the first woman to win a Nobel Prize, and the first woman to earn a doctorate in Europe. Pearl S. Buck (1892-1973) won the Nobel Prize for Literature with her novels about American and Asian culture. Today we have Oprah Winfrey an actress though she is more known as a talk show host and winner of several Emmy Awards. Other achievers include women like Shirley Jackson, the former head of the United States Nuclear Regulatory Commission. Helen Keller (1880-1968) a woman left deaf, mute, and blinded by a childhood disease. This woman went on to become an expert, author and lecturer educating nations on behalf of others with similar disabilities. She didn't allow the box of disability hold her down.

Rejection is not an excuse

The next space is yours. Ms/Mrs/Miss . . . . What will history have to say about you? Remember it is never too late to make deposits into your future. How will you be remembered, what mark will you like to leave behind? When people come in contact with you, what do they see? Do they rue the day they met you or are they forever grateful you came into their life. History awaits your impact, in your home, your place of work, community, nation and even the world. It might be difficult but it is possible. At the end the reward is great! Your children will call you great, your spouse's heart will trust in you. Even as we know that you cannot control another person, if they refuse to esteem you, then relax because history will remember you. Don't be limited rather limit your limitations and reach for the sky.

Two

You can't keep a good woman down

A Woman's Story

The idea of be seen and not heard is an age long experience of women. They were deemed to be good just for one thing . . . maybe two depending on their nationality. Their traditional role was to procreate and rear children, clean the house and cook. In some other societies, women had the added responsibility of being used as underpaid and over exploited farm hands. In those times, only few women dared to break the silence and step out of line and those who dared were viewed negatively and named. . . . bra burners, man haters, rude, un-submissive, feminist and domineering were among the unpleasant titles they got. Those in religious circles were mainly named after Jezebel the wicked witch from the ancient times who over the years has come to symbolize vocal and controlling women. Though you don't hear those labels so loud today, they are still non-verbally communicated to women with strong personalities especially women who are self-confident or high achievers.

In the story from which the principles in this book are extracted, I invite readers to observe the life of an ordinary woman who became unforgettable. As we explore we can make deduction and understand what she had and what she did to earn such an accolade as an *Unforgettable Woman.* On this dark evening, it was no different as a day which started like any other ended in a remarkable way and made its

8

way into the history books. A nameless woman, despised for being of loose morals in one account₁ while another version reviled her for being wasteful₂ became unforgettable. It brought a shift in the way she was seen and described. It gave her a new story and separated her from the crowd. She was not the most qualified, neither was she the prettiest or fairest but she made it into the rank of the *Unforgettables.* This woman dared to break out of a cultural, traditional and religious mould, disregard all the negative comments and followed her heart, her dreams and desires.

The Dinner Party Where it All Started

One faithful evening, a nameless woman heard that Simon, one of the wealthy men in the town where she lived was hosting a highly esteemed religious dignitary to dinner at his house. Simon put on a well laid out dinner with no expense spared as he had invited a lot of his friends and colleagues who were highly placed in government. The atmosphere he succeeded in creating was relaxed and cheerful with a lot of talking, banter and loud bursts of laughter around the room.

Everyone wanted to talk to the dinner guest, some wanted to sit by his right and some on his left. Some questioned him on how he spent his money and how he managed to pay his bills. Others wanted to hear about his trips around the different regions, the people he had met along the way and those he helped. Some of his travel companions who were at the dinner with him regaled the others with stories of how he instructed them to open the mouth of a fish and get money to pay their taxes! The main highlight for the other guests was the mind-blowing speech he was known to make as his theories were usually laced with parables.

This dinner guest was no ordinary man. He was rather young, in his early thirties but he was very influential and eloquent. He was a good crowd magnet and his words had people thinking for hours and days questioning their beliefs, policies and principles. He was a natural leader with a huge number of fans as people readily followed him. Though many liked him but like everything else, some didn't. Some groups were constantly looking for ways to trip him up, waiting and hoping for him to make a mistake. This all-important man came to dinner at Simon's place and it was as usual an all men's affair. The women only appeared at such meetings to serve the food, fill up the wine jars and clean the spills.

Dinner was served and all the men settled down to the very serious business of eating when suddenly there was a loud bang as the door swung shut. Everyone looked up towards the door and there stood a woman holding something in her hand that looked like a small flowery box. The woman who looked extremely nervous and unsure of herself seemed to heave a sigh and taking a step she walked slowly into the room. In surprise, the men who recognized her from the community began to think aloud and whisper to each other with some dismissing her because of her past and others irritated at her audacity.

". . . Maybe she is bringing part of the meal to be served, but that box is too small to contain anything" one of the men reasoned.

". . . Maybe she came to see Simon, the owner of the house . . . aaahh! She has passed him by" another said.

"What's up?" They wondered and whispered to each other. As realization set in, some of them became indignant and began to seethe.

. . . Oh my! Exclaimed one of the more vocal guests, "She's walking straight to the dinner guest"

"Who let her in here" another lamented" . . . what is this woman doing gate crashing our meeting" they argued. "Does she not know it's a men's meeting" added yet another. "Does she not know her place" more of them raged and fumed under their breath.

Without hesitation, she seemed to make a bee line for her by now obvious target, the dinner guest who seemed to watch the proceedings with keen interest without uttering a word. When the woman got to him, he looked up at her, only then did she fully reveal the parcel in her hand, which was a small alabaster box. Now, all eyes were fully on her.

"Hey! What are you doing" someone shouted at her as she took a small object and began to crack it against the side of the box. Suddenly the box broke and a sweet aroma escaped from the cracked box filling the room. Then she finally went OTT—over the top and poured what was left in the box on the head of the dinner guest as a sign of appreciation, respect and love. . . . Ohhh! The men chorused. They seemed to have had enough and lapsed into an eerie silence as they waited for the dinner guest's reaction.

If her arrival in the room shocked the guests, then his reaction certainly put them in their place and perplexed them even more. Ignoring their indignation, he took a deep breath, inhaled slowly as he savoured the scent of the perfume. He then lifted up his head looking directly at her and for the first time spoke up and said *"woman, you are unforgettable."* Okay, this paraphrase is mine but what he really did was instruct the men that everywhere they spoke about him and his awesome deeds they must talk about her$_3$. In modern English terms what he was really saying was that from that day onward, for that remarkable act she was to become unforgettable, etched into history. To say the men were shocked is a mild understatement as they expected him to give out to her, berate her or even banish her from the room but he did none of those. Instead, her actions gained his approval and caused him to defend her openly in front of her opponents. He built a memorable relationship with her. One without borders of control, traditions, gender inequality, power struggle or boxed in positions created by society. He gave her the one thing that makes women feel fulfilled in relationships.

Three

What Women Want in Relationship

The joy and excitement experienced by women when they find that person who knows how to appreciate a woman, or make her feel valued and good about herself. The timely thank you an individual receives without having to prompt the other person or words that send the message that she is appreciated and understood. When the significant others in their life actually act as if they see and appreciate the effort women put in to make the home work, or the employer who recognizes and rewards their hard work, dedication and initiative. That person who doesn't take her contributions for granted or as an act of duty. That is exactly what many women are looking for. Someone, with whom they feel special, valued and wanted. A person who sees what the woman can be and not what she used to be, someone who is part of their future not a constant reminder of their past failings. Someone who defends her publicly and fights her corner with friends, in-laws, out-laws and even with the kids.

Operating From a Position of Power

Women can operate from a position of power or from a position of need. The position of power is a place of confidence where the woman knows her value and worth and then everything around her sees and identifies it while the other is a needy and disempowering position where she waits for others to see and say that she is special.

It is quite difficult to make someone feel what they don't feel about themselves. If as a woman you don't feel you are special, if you don't feel you have something special nothing anyone outside yourself says will convince you otherwise. Even when they seem convinced, it is usually short lived and in need of constant affirmation. This is one of the main reasons many women have problematic relationships. They give their power away to others because it portrays her as needy.

The woman in our story had something special and precious, she knew its worth and value. She didn't need something or someone outside herself to tell her that. What makes this argument difficult is that human beings more especially women are relational beings who get their sense of value and worth in relation to what the other is or isn't. It rekindles the age old debate of the chicken and the egg and which one came first. Do women feel special because the people they encounter say they are or are women special and then the people they meet see the special qualities in them? If first we focus on what we can change, what we can control then whichever one comes first appears irrelevant. The emphasis should be which position restores a woman's power, which position puts her in control and in the driver's sit of her life. Remember, you cannot change another person though many women still invest a lot of effort trying to do just that! When you change something about the way you operate then things around you will adjust to that change. It is just a matter of time and patience but the change is inevitable because life responds. It's like the weather, once it is winter, the jackets come out, the lights stay on longer and the heating comes on. When it is summer and it is hotter, we lose the jacket, and put on lighter clothes. Life will respond to your change.

You cannot change another person. The only person you can change is you

Role playing and metaphors usually help me see clearer because many people are usually smarter about what others should do than they are about themselves. So let's look at another woman's issue and learn from her. Imagine a brilliant and confident woman gets captured for six months, she is isolated and called a cat every day. Will she suddenly grow fur, meow like a cat and slurp milk? Seriously, no way, it's not even remotely possible unless you zap her or hypnotize her. You know why, it is simply because she is human, she is a woman, she knows it and her body knows it. My question to you is what do you know about yourself, who are you, what price will you place on yourself if you were to go on a public auction (don't do it!). On a serious note, what price will you say you are worth bearing in mind the woman? What do you think and say about yourself.

Change is Possible

You cannot rise higher than the level of what you genuinely think and believe about yourself. Even when well-intentioned people try to convince you otherwise, most times people just think they are lying or being deceptive for personal gains. It is however not all doom and gloom because change is possible. Self-doubt didn't just happen one day, it developed through a process and as such anyone experiencing it can definitely overcome it. Self-doubt starts from past experiences, where negative incidences are held as ones sole truth. It comes from having a tunnel vision concerning one's life and experiences. Truly some peoples past experiences are painful and horrific and some happened during childhood in trusting and helpless situation.

Some women might have been abused as children or maybe you are someone who never got proper education and as such have always felt disadvantaged in groups. For some women it might be that you have seen everyone in your family achieve while you remain struggling to make ends meet. I don't know what you have been through or how bad it is and it is not even a "whose situation is worse" competition. Whatever your unique situation is, whatever happened, so long as you are alive you can do something about it if you want to and if you put your mind to it. It will not be easy but I can assure you that for your peace of mind, for your mental health it will definitely be worth it. Especially when it involves hurts from the past, the motivation should be to not allow the past affect more of ones future and most definitely not the lives of your kids. It means getting off that merry go round of pain and hurt and saying it stops here! Maybe it is a ten per cent, twenty or even the whole one hundred per cent change; no matter how small or big don't you think it is worth it. I sincerely hope you will be prepared to work towards a change in your circumstance even if it is a ten per cent positive change rather than staying stuck.

The main challenge is that many women are waiting . . . just waiting for a chance, they are waiting for change to happen to them. They are waiting for people to do it for them, for absentee dads, or mums who are worried about their own lives and have their own problems to come and fix them. They are waiting for a society that is steeped in recession and playing the big game of politics and Russian roulette with policies, State assets and funds affecting people's lives and livelihood. *Becoming Unforgettable* is about how you roll up your sleeve and get under the hood of what your life has become and is tending to every day and begin to work. It's about getting into the drivers sit of your life. *The attitude of change is, I can, I want to and I am going to. It is about your decisions, choices and belief* Maybe everyone else has been driving you around, taking you places you don't want to go. It is time to get out of that bus and take the wheels of your own life. Remember the popular saying; 'the journey of a thousand miles begins with one step'. The first step to change is an "I can, I want to and I am going to" attitude. It is about the three I's. . . . I . . . I . . . I. It's all about you, your decisions, your choices and your belief.

Women and the Martyr Syndrome

Many women today are on the brink of a mental collapse. Tired, bogged down frustrated and just about exhausted. You see women with this double existence where on the outside they appear okay and on the inside they are falling apart from too much responsibility. Why do women feel this great sense of responsibility, who sent you? Many years ago, I was having a misunderstanding with my husband and I was giving out and listing all the things I do in the house, all the things I do for the kids and all the things I do for him. Does that sound familiar to you? Well he helped me that day because he asked me a question in the heat of the row, he said "who sent you." I did a quick double take, I blinked and spluttered but you know what,

I didn't have an answer because I sent myself. My interpretation of my "role" of what a good dutiful wife and mother should be sent me. My need to be seen as a good wife and mother made me do things I didn't really want to do. He totally changed my life and relationship with people. From that day I became conscious of my motive because if you do things because you want to not just because it makes you look good then you will not be gaging for appreciation from the other person.

As simple as it might be, it is very important because it is the root of bitterness in many relationships where women feel unappreciated and unloved. In African circles, we call that "eye service". How many things are you doing so that others will think good of you? Many relationships stress lies in that singular factor because it comes loaded with disappointment and hurt. The reason for your actions should be because you love the other person not because you want them to love you. That way you don't get hurt and disappointed. Motive is really important but we will discuss it further in later chapters.

One comment I get a lot from women of all colours, sizes and built is a long list of what people made them do. What they have to do for their children their spouse or what their partners made them do. It is usually a litany of how . . . they have to clean up after their partners, pick up clothes and trousers which are left lying on the floor or across the foot of the bed. Many talk about their partners being 'useless' in the kitchen, they claim he can't even wash his own shirts, he can't pack his own travel case or find the second pair of his socks . . . Take a moment and think about it, if you were not there doing all those things do you really, really think they will not be able to do it themselves? Seriously! Before you came on the scene how did they survive, if you were to drop dead today, what do you seriously think will happen. They will survive and unfortunately the way people are if there is someone else there doing the job they will not struggle to take it over from you. No matter

Reflection

Are you what you do or do you do the things you do because of who you are?

how poorly people can do a job they can do it. So maybe it's time to let them. Let the kids, let your colleagues, your spouse—let them do it to the best of their ability. After all, many hands they say make work light!

Who sent you, really, who asked you to do all those things, I mean actually asked you . . . the first time you did it, were you asked or did you take it upon yourself. Many women have become Martyr's in their homes; they have become superwoman where they are everything to everyone and nothing to themself. They have become the answer to everyone's problem except their own. Women naturally strive to satisfy what others have said, to fit into the boxes that women have been placed. They accept roles unquestioning to the point that they are not aware of any other way. They unwittingly take on the victim role in their own homes where their actions are no longer by personal choice but as a rule.

Co-dependent women

The issue of identity is still a major one for many women as some interchange role for who they are. When asked who are you many women answer with whose wife they are, whose mother they are, some answer with the job they do. "What am I, where am I in my life, who am I" were three questions a woman asked in tears as she tried to untangle what her life had become. 'I can't see me in my life' she cried quietly. The challenge is that the roles women function in and occupy are vital for the smooth running of the home, however, if all that were taken away then what is left. The absence of a suitable answer to this question pushes many women to make choices they know are detrimental to them.

When an adult woman shows a lack of good sense of self, personal boundaries, and the resources to create the type of life that honours her but instead she merely strives to live up to other's expectations or live a lifestyle designed to impress others then such a woman can be called a co-dependent woman. This dependency can be on the children, spouse or partner even a colleague at work. Meanwhile, she of course ignores her own needs and wants and in fact many co-dependent women are hardly aware

"A sick woman is not loved and a dead woman is easily replaced"

of their own needs and wants or have chosen to ignore and suppress them. They are typically used to looking outward and catering to others demands. In fact, co-dependent women often look to a partner, their roles, and or a lifestyle for a sense of identity.

A friend told me an allegory, she said "a sick woman is not loved and a dead woman is easily replaced." I went uhmmmm, because it was very troubling and deep. Just recently in the news in Ireland, they mentioned that a number of women were feeling under pressure managing life and home pressures. The number of women still doing the laundry for their twenty years old will absolutely amaze you. Who sent you to pick up the clothes of your ten year old off the floor, when he comes back from school. A child who doesn't put his chocolates in his nostrils and can play any new X Box games that you the parent is completely clueless about, you feel he or she can't hang up their own clothes, make their beds and empty their lunch bags? Many women take on that level of involvement in the lives of those around them to feel relevant and wanted. Sometimes women claim that the recipient cannot do it themselves but they will never learn as long as the need is not constantly presented to them. We are as guilty as the people we seemingly help because we enable them all in the hope of gaining a sense of self-worth but we incapacitate them by those actions. Is it easy to get a ten year old to pick up after themselves, no way! I am living through that now but some days are better than others when I come back home from work and everything is done then I go happy days . . ., and other days I have to ask them *again* to do it. Can you love the people in your life enough to let them grow up or do you need them to like you so much you are willing to risk disempowering them. Co-dependency is if you encourage others to need you because it makes you feel valued and necessary.

A friend used to say "don't complain about what you permit". I really thought he was heartless and un-empathetic about my circumstances, but he honestly did me a great favour because that is one principle I live my life by. It stopped me from feeling sorry for myself. It stopped me from taking on the victim role and having a one woman pity party where I am the host and only guest! I stopped concentrating on what I perceived people to be doing to me and my focus changed to what I am *permitting*

Don't Complain About What You Permit

people to do to me. That way, the power returns to me and I can control and stop what I don't like. For example I remove myself from abusive or unprofitable friendships. I stay where I am celebrated and appreciated and not with people or in places where I am tolerated. We will expand on some of these principles in later chapters of this book and see how you can make these ideas practical in your life.

As with everything in life, there are always extreme cases but most times, people play a big part in allowing others mete out all kinds of treatment to them. If you have ever witnessed an argument with a sales personnel in shops where they have to call the shop manager, one thing the manager says is, please can you keep your voice down. 'I can't really resolve this if you speak in a raised voice.' In essence, she is saying no matter what is wrong here I will not permit you to shout at me or my staff or intimidate me even when she is secretly intimidated. Maybe you can try it with your kids, or with your spouse the next time they are screaming at you, just say I am sorry I cannot really hear clearly in the midst of raised voices while at the same time you keep your tone level and low. It cools the tone of the argument and forces it down.

My car is usually full on Friday evenings as I take my two sons and their friends to the kids club and of course, the screaming is unbelievable as you can expect with seven kids in a car for a fifteen minutes ride! Though many of my friends think I am mental for doing that. Once the crying starts and they are trying to tell me what happened, I simple say 'look love I can't really hear you in that crying voice, so if you need me to do something about it you need to speak to me in a calm voice and tell me what happened and it usually works because she wants to be heard and understood.

Please hear me! No one can make you do things even when brute force and fear is involved. *Not making* This is however in normal everyday relationship *a choice is* not where there are very unequal power levels *a choice in* for example when a forty years old man abuses a *itself* child. Many women chose one form of pain over the other. For example, the fear and pain of being alone is so terrifying for some women that they stay in the pain of being physically abused, raped and emotionally controlled. For some it is the fear of what people will say and for some it is the unpaid bills and sometimes a combination of fears. There is a popular saying that you can force a horse to the river but you cannot force the horse to drink. Please! People can't make you do what you don't want to. A lot of issues in life are about the choices people make and not making a choice is a choice in itself. Therein lies you power. As Albert Einstein said, Insanity is doing the same thing over and over again expecting different results. Please if the result you are getting is not okay for you change your strategy.

Who holds the power reins in your life, is it your kids, your partner, your mum, your dad, the society or even friends, who is pulling your strings. In some cases it is peoples past experiences, the abuse, lack of education, institutions, systems and their policies or even the way your immediate family have treated you in the past. Who pulls your fear strings? What are you afraid of and what are you doing and bearing to hide that fear?

A Woman and a Person

How many duties have you taken upon yourself expecting to be appreciated and rewarded? Remember "do not complain about what you permit". Many women maintain the stereotype that society has put on them and though they can multitask, many chose to multitask in specific roles recognized as 'female' roles.

The minute you allow yourself to be boxed into a stereotype you stop being unique, you compromise your individuality and difference. Remember everyone is not made to be the same.

Stereotype stops you being unique and compromises your individuality

What choice will you make today, will you allow people, life and circumstances tell you who you are, what you can and cannot do or be, or are you going to be you. A person, an individual with choices and actualize your full potential. The increasing double existence operated by many women has been proving a hugely emotional challenge and strain for many. One minute it is the cheerful woman and the next minute it is the sad, tired, unfulfilled, spent and unappreciated woman you have. Individual motivation is really vital, the reason you do the things you do is really important to maintaining ones sanity especially for us women. Remember, "A sick woman is not loved and a dead woman is easily replaced". As the Irish say, 'mind yourself'. I love it! Ladies mind yourselves.

Are you willing to take a chance to improve the conditions of your life? Just like the woman from our story you can go from an ordinary nameless existence to become remarkable. You can definitely be unforgettable if you want to. You can increase your circle of influence and affect a room, house or nation full of people and be unforgettable. You can affect your fella's life or your children's lives and be unforgettable. There is a way you touch people's lives and they are affected positively and no matter how high they go or what they accomplish, they will always remember you. You can have this too. You can be unforgettable. If that is what you want for yourself and the women in your life then read on.

The rest of *becoming Unforgettable* deals with attributes and skills women can cultivate and develop to lead a truly impactful and influential life. This woman changed the atmosphere in that meeting and you can to. You can change society starting from where you are right now. They say change a woman and you change a whole society. Your reach as a woman is great. You are a ball of influence. Read my next book on the Female-Man on who a woman truly is. Combined with these qualities you will be unstoppable. Remember you didn't get here in one day, it will also take a process to bring your change but be glad and hopeful because change is possible.

If the result you are getting is not good change your strategy

Today is the future you talked about five, ten years ago, you can start today and begin to make new deposits into your next future years. Make new deposits into how your life will be in the next five to ten years. Start practicing principles and developing new ways of being and you will see your change. Many people think it's too late but I assure you, it's never too late to turn around. If it's not working do something about it because today is the first day of the rest of your life.

Principles for living

- You cannot rise higher than the level of what you genuinely think and believe about yourself.
- No one can make you feel what you don't genuinely feel about yourself.
- Don't complain about what you permit.
- The first step for change is an "I can, I want to and I am going to" attitude.
- Change is all about you, your decisions, your choices and your belief.
- If the result you are getting is not okay for you change your strategy.
- It's never too late to turn around.
- Why you do the things you do is really important to helping you keep your sanity.
- Whoever controls your perception of yourself controls your life.
- People are usually wiser about what others should do than what they themselves should do.
- As long as one is alive and well change is possible if you want to and if you put your mind to it.
- Not making a choice is a choice in itself.

PART TWO

The Twelve Qualities of an Unforgettable Woman

12 Qualities of an Unforgettable Woman

The woman in the story had some qualities which I am going to highlight and hopefully, you will see something that will motivate and challenge you to be the best you alive and the very best you possible. Not a suppressed, oppressed or even a repressed you but an alive and kicking you. You know the way they say you can't keep a good 'woman' down, well sisters, let that woman be you. Pardon me that I call you Sisters even if you are black, white or in-between, as my colleague from work jokes, 'you are my sister from another mother'. Since the world and people didn't make you they cannot unmake you unless you allow them because your destiny is not in the hands of man. What you are and what you can be is not in the hands of others. Please don't let the world, society or even what people say, think or expect of you limit you or kill your dreams and desires. Live! Live!! Live!!! Remember, you have a right to be here, you have a right to live and a right to life. More importantly, you have a right to be happy and you deserve that happiness.

I want to encourage you to keep reading because you are getting to the juicy part of *Becoming Unforgettable*. The woman's story in the original text was written as an example from which we can be instructed, corrected and it is also to provide principles for the perfection of humans1. Each story, each parable, each occurrence encapsulates principles for effective daily living. It establishes the order and more importantly it can build up, empower and establish people in their purpose especially when it has been undermined just like the purpose and place of women has been subverted by tradition and those in power. From this nameless woman's life I have extracted twelve qualities that can support and inspire women to increase their circle of influence to an *Unforgettable* existence. It is time for your change. It's your move to becoming Unforgettable.

Four

Bold but Beautiful

An Unforgettable Woman Is Bold

Individuals are to a large extent influenced by their upbringing which in turn impacts on their expectations, beliefs and world view. From childhood people are easily conditioned to suppress their natural inclinations. At birth the first set of words spoken out to children are the soothing sshhh . . . sound which caring adults proffer while trying to calm and sooth children or cajole them to stop crying. Children themselves very quickly learn what they can or cannot do as their early days are packed with a series of don'ts . . . don't touch, don't cry, don't stamp your feet, don't bite . . . . Even when they are crying from hunger or they are uncomfortable from sitting in a soaked nappy! People automatically still say sshhhh . . . stopping them from expressing their feelings in the way they know how. Such actions programme children early to suppress what they really want to do and on getting older they are faced with the difficulty of no longer trusting their natural inclination and intuition. People end up learning early to look towards others to affirm them and to tell them what is right to do. This is one of the biggest losses of society and families because of the way human beings are wired especially women who are more intuitive and have knowledge that ordinarily they can't explain logically.

In the republic of Ireland where I presently reside the more common application of the word bold has a negative connotation especially for children. Its commonplace usage indicates the child in question is not listening, is causing a lot of disturbance to order or is basically not conforming to directions from those in authority and it usually epitomizes someone "doing something bad".

In its original context however, being bold means to be fearless and daring, to have courage and be willing to challenge situations. It includes being able to carry on ignoring feelings of timidity, fear, shame and or shyness when present. Being bold is a positive and desirable attribute which comes in handy for everyone at different times in their lives. It is what enables individuals even in the face of fear to do the very thing they are afraid of doing. It encourages people to press on to accomplish what they want even when they are quaking inside, feeling foolish or even intimidated.

> *Being bold is being daring and having the courage and will to challenge your circumstances*

Many destinies and dreams have been truncated because of how people respond to fear. Though fear is a very common enemy for many, its main power and destruction rests in how far people allow it to control and rule their lives. Life has these boxes which it tries to use to contain people. Sometimes it is other individuals who try to curtail people and as such individuals grow up living within those stipulated boxes. Women are the worse served with boxes because in every sphere of life she has been told what, who and how to be a woman. To have the heart and guts . . . to dare to step out of such constricting boxes is a completely freeing and exhilarating experience, a place of possibilities and opportunities for an unforgettable woman.

The boxed up mentality

Boxes are used to confine, condone off or set boundaries. They can serve a dual purpose of keeping things in or out. In other words, some boxes are necessary and they can be good or bad, helpful or damaging. When people are told how to be, what they can or cannot do, it serves as an invisible boundary that can either keeps them in or out. It can leave them protected or isolated. So the first thing is an awareness of the boxes in our lives. What is its purpose, how did it or how did they come about. There are boxes that are good and even vital for a two year old but for a twenty year old they are ridiculous. What we have today is that many individuals have all kinds of boxes around their lives and the sad thing is just like a baby in the womb, you cannot grow bigger than the boxes in your life.

Human beings are creatures of choice. There is always the choice of going left, right or standing still; going up, down or stagnating; there is positive, negative and even neutral. When faced with a box which can be any form of limitation or limiting factor, people react in three possible ways. Now if you are very creative you might be able to think up more options and that's why metaphors and analogies are great. It paints a picture that people can easily relate with and understand. It makes it easier for people to see where they fit. People react to limitations in three possible ways.

Those Who Live Within the Box

These are people who know their limitations and make no attempt to challenge it. They think impossibilities and believe wholly what others say about them. They don't think they are making a choice to stay down rather they believe they have no choice. They usually feel like the victims of circumstances and believe their lives would have been better if they only had . . ., *that space is* an endless list of really good reasons.

However, there are many other people who have those same limitations in their lives and yet have gone ahead and succeeded in life. These women are completely immobilized by the thoughts and fear of what they cannot do, what they cannot have and where they cannot go. Change is not usually an option they consider rather they stay resigned to fate.

Those who carry the box with them

These are women who question and challenge the boxes instilled by others, their traditions, culture and commandments[1]. They see those boxes as limitations and they desire more because they know they can have more. Such women crave for and even plan and pursue their dreams. However, many of their efforts end up unaccomplished because they are easily discouraged by circumstances and opposition. They are people who have a constant inner voice and critique that tells them what they cannot do. It gives them good reasons why they cannot do it, why they cannot succeed by focusing on and over emphasizing their weaknesses. They are individuals who break out of the box but are never completely free of it because they carry their boxes as baggage and are weighed down by it. These are women who still have fear playing havoc with their minds$_2$. Carrying your past hurts into your present will limit your tomorrow. To be a truly unforgettable woman, you have to be bold enough to leave the past in yesterday. That is where true victory and freedom is borne.

Those who break the box

There are people who like the incredible hulk character David Banner break out of the box. They see those boxes as limitations that can be surmounted. They dislodge every internal argument and challenge the norms. They do not take societies norms as their standard. They are not afraid of what has not been done before and in the face of real fear, they allow their convictions see them through.

"Failure is not a person it is an event"

Unfortunately, there are very few people who attain unto this level. They are the real dreamers those who dare, they take risks and are not afraid of failing. For them failure is not a person it is an event that educates them of what not to do. They see failure as a lesson in what doesn't work. This is the substance true achievers, leaders, pioneers and entrepreneurs are made of. To truly succeed, you have to learn to break all the boxes and limitation.

Decision Determines Destination

Your decisions will determine where and how you end up. If you want to influence your outcome in life the first place to work on is the decisions you make. I repeat it because it is so important—*not making a decision is a decision itself.* At the end of the day, the choice is yours alone. You decide what will make you happy, you decide what and how much you can bear. You decide what dreams you are willing to pursue. You decide what you are willing to let go of and you decide what you are willing to live or die for.

Your decisions will determine your outcome in life

Let me ask you, what version of yourself will you wake up to in the morning and admire what you have become. We never fully arrive until the day we pass away as we are all in the process of being made . . . in the process of becoming. So what variety of you will you respect and love. If you were not you, will you be attracted to you. Take a moment and think about it. I always ask the groups I work with during my motivation classes how they can increase their worth. How can you increase your economic, physical and spiritual worth and how can you increase your circle of influence. What can you do to remedy that, what can you do to improve your position. Remember, it's never too late!

Becoming Unforgettable is me breaking out of the box and limitations in my life. This is me daring in the face of impossibilities, challenges and practical difficulties. It is me pursing my dreams and if you are reading this book today then it just goes to prove that we can make it happen. Dreams can still come true but first you must dare to dream. You cannot rise above the magnitude and quality of your dreams. So dear Sisters, dear friends, dear unforgettable women dream big, it is the one place you can travel without spending money, without needing a visa, childcare or permission. Your dreams are there at your service to work for you. Please use it.

Fear the Great Opponent of Boldness

It is difficult to comprehend the impact fear has on many lives until you see what it is depriving people of. If you were not afraid what would you be doing with your life? If you knew you couldn't fail, what will you do? That dear friend . . . is exactly what fear is robing and depriving you of. It is a major hindrance to many women's lives as it prevents them from progressing the way they want to and from doing the things they really want to do. It keeps the desires of a lot of women as dreams rather than reality. The fact is that fear is not unique to women as men are affected by it as well. However, a lot of men exhibit more boldness in the face of their fears and they are much better at hiding it or not giving in to it.

> *You cannot rise above the magnitude and quality of your dreams.*

Fear is an intangible force that brings feelings of dread, terror and ultimately causes people to hesitate and finally stops them from doing what they really want to do. It shows up as the inner voice telling you what you can or can't do. It screams so loud that people actually believe it. For the many thousands of people who wonder how their fear started, there are many suggestions proffered about how fear develops. Some erroneously believe fear just came on them suddenly; some others believe the medical model and see fear as a state of mental ill health while some see it as spiritual. It actually can be all those things and more.

How Fear Operates

Fear has a definite pattern of operating. It can start as a simple thought that seems to pop into the mind or inner world and many people discount it and allow it to stay in their mind. Then the mind acts as a nourished soil for the thought, in fact fear thoughts are like seeds to a farmer and the mind is the mechanism for the growth of thoughts. It processes the thought sometimes based on past experiences, what people have said and the general information available to you at the moment or in the circumstance.

Full blown fear is like pictures in the mind of what could happen and it is produced as part of the thinking process. What fear does is that it stacks up a series of thoughts as evidence for what is going to happen. As is popularly quoted, F.E.A.R is **F**alse **E**vidence **A**ppearing **R**eal. This thought begins to grow stronger and stronger till the person gets to the point that the thought now takes control of the individuals mind. The human mind does its part of feeding the fear by producing pictures of what will happen. Usually, those pictures depict negative, scary and horrible outcomes.

The thing with fear is that it can be quite tormenting$_2$. As Franklin D. Roosevelt said at his first inaugural address the "only thing we have to fear is fear itself". So it is really important for us to recognize fear and deal with it. You have to watch your thinking, anything that comes into your mind with disturbing feelings. You can tackle it by looking for a positive thought and use it to erase that horrible thought$_3$ the same way you will over write a CD. This is not just positive thinking, you are fighting for your sanity

If you don't think you will stink, so start by getting rid of stinking thinking.

and your peace of mind. Would you rather allow a lie fester in your mind and paralyse you or would you pick on the truth in your life and focus on it. You decide.

Those who have never experienced real limiting fear might not understand the enormity of its effect on a life bound by fear, a mind where fear plays havoc day and night. They might even see it as hilarious but those whose lives have been tormented by things only visible to them will understand. I mean if you have not left your house for the past ten years and you are under a self inflicted solitary confinement from what you fear you will understand. Living in fear is a terrible place to be. It can turn a happy, healthy man or woman into a mere shadow of him/herself. Yet studies show that eighty five per cent of what we fear never really happens. I want to encourage you, you can win over that fear, no matter how long it has been going on you can win. Fear works by keeping you bound in his circle but you can break out of that circle the minute you start thinking and challenging your thoughts. Remember *"if you don't think you will stink"* so start by getting rid of every self-limiting and stinking thinking.

The Power of Fear

- It is based on the assumption and acceptance of false evidence without proof.
- It worries about something in the future that might not really happen
- Fear works in secrecy and thrives in silence
- It grows through the imagination
- It produces feelings of powerlessness
- It demonstrates and thrives in ignorance
- It is destroyed by the knowledge of the truth[4]

Practical Strategy to Deal with Fear

1. Challenge unwanted thoughts

It is really important that you do not ignore thoughts that paint a picture of what you don't want in your mind or head. The first step is to question the thought. Is it true, whose truth is it, where is it from—mum, dad, society, tradition, culture where? Then ask yourself if that is what you really want. Remember, whatsoever is good think on these things.[3]

2. Treat unwanted thoughts as intruders

Treat those damaging thoughts the same way you will treat an intruder trying to break into your house. Most modern houses today have an alarm system that alerts you when someone without legal rights is trying to gain access into your house. In your day to day existence you will make every attempt to throw the intruder out, you resist them and deny them entrance into your house. What most people do is to look for what has triggered their alarm. Now if you take that much care of your physical property that is made by human hands and can easily be replaced, what about your mind, your whole self and your peace of mind. Is it not worth the effort for you to stand guard over your mind to disallow those negative, tormenting thoughts which I call illegal thoughts from coming in?

The danger is that if such thoughts are left unchallenged they can come in, encroach on a susceptible mind and take permanent residence. Once they get a hold of one's mind, they produce beliefs which with time ends up reproducing what the person sees and believes[5]. At this stage, you have what you fear producing like a self-fulfilling prophecy.

3. Identify your fear triggers

Many people feel powerless against their thoughts as if things just willy-nilly come into their minds and stay there. That is not the case most times, what I encourage is to trace back in your thoughts and see what triggered the feeling in you, was it a movie, something someone said, a friend is getting married and suddenly you are afraid you will die an old spinster, the triggers are real and very close by. If you catch the feeling early enough then go back over the last twenty four hours you will detect your fear triggers. Just retrace your train of thoughts.

4. Replace the fear thought with what you hope for

Challenge those thoughts and replace them with your truth which should be what you want to see happening, not what you fear will happen. Remember whatsoever is good, whatsoever is true, whatsoever is admirable, think on these things[3]. Statistics shows that over eighty per cent of the things we fear never actually happen. So use your thinking wisely and make *You become what you think[5]* it work for you because you become what you think[5]. How do people go from mild anger to raging mad? It's in the thinking process. People think deeply on what happened and this affects what they are feeling. The more aggressively you think the thoughts the deeper and stronger your feelings will be.

5. Break your fear habits and patterns

Studies show that anything you do continuously for seven days becomes a habit. Unfortunately, once habits are formed they are not so easy to break by human efforts alone. Some simple practical steps that will help include interrupting the negative thought in the middle. One valuable lesson I learnt many years ago is that you cannot talk and think at the same time. One stops for the other. Try it and see. So fear thrives best when people remain silent[6]. As the thought begins to play out and fill your mind, find a quiet place so they will not take you to the loony bin! Speak out the opposing word or situation to what you are afraid of. For example if it is the fear of death then speak out and say I shall not die[7].

Boldness in the 21st Century Woman

Boldness is not the absence of fear rather it is you challenging what you fear. It is a decision not to allow fear limit you. Being bold is the point where individuals stand by their convictions, the point of decision where they say "I am going to do this" whatever your "*this*" is. Whether it is pursuing your dreams, contributing at a meeting, applying for a job, attending an interview, meeting new people or saying hello to someone you fancy. It can be a big step in people's social development. The best way to deal with fear is to do what you fear. The minute you dare, the very thing you fear loses its power against you. Think about it, what is the worst thing that can happen, they will simply say no to you and no has not killed anyone yet. It is the way you react to the 'No' that kills many people. It is important to be aware that being bold is different from being aggressive which is a negative attribute. Many people however erroneously mistake and interchange being bold, daring and confident as a cover for being nasty.

Boldness is not the absence of fear

Consider the woman in our story, a woman just like you and I, she probably had her heart in her mouth from nerves but that didn't stop her. She kept on going, her knees were probably knocking with her mouth gone dry with fear. Her heart would have been beating too fast and too loud yet she kept on going. She heard the snide remarks they were making about her past, because most of them knew her from the neighborhood and they knew the horrible things she had done before yet that didn't stop her. Remember carrying your past into your present will weigh down your future and it can even stop you. An unforgettable woman choses her moments, she knows when to be daring and when to let go. Remember what they say "don't sweat the small stuff".

35

Don't Be Enslaved By Your Fears

The fear of past mistakes, embarrassments and shortcoming showing up in their present life or new circle of friends is one major source of concern for many people. The thoughts of the shame and embarrassment makes many people hide away and it is the very reason blackmailers' succeed. However, as we have seen in the movies and real life situations with various footballers and movie stars, paying blackmailers never works because they come back for more and more and more. They ultimately turn you into their slave for as long as they want. There might be things you have done or are going through that you are afraid will come up again, things from your past you would prefer no one finds out or remembers but you can't let that stop you because at the end of the day, only you lose. Think about it, these people who you are afraid of, who intimidate and stop you actually still carry on with their lives while yours is filled with unfulfilled dreams and desires.

"Someone who has not made a mistake is a person who has not accomplished much"

Nobody is worth giving up your dreams for neither is any fear. The woman from our story had a sordid past yet she made the move to get what she wanted. My challenge to you today is that you make a move, go for it, don't let anything or anyone stop you, it's your life and it's your dream. The main thing that can stop you is fear; fear of failure, fear of what people will say, the fear of making a mistake. But a wise man once said, show me someone who has not made a mistake and I will show you someone who has not accomplished much.

Fear is a very unhealthy basis for a relationship, either at work, sexual relationship, marriage, or even friendship. For example if the sight of some people arouses fear in you even the sound of their voice makes you afraid. I will say that if fear is the predominant feeling you get in the relationship then there is already a problem at the foundation$_8$. Don't start a relationship with someone who arouses feelings of fear and trepidation in you. Love and respect are the best basis for an employer/employee or romantic relationship, even the relationship with your children should be love motivated and not fear driven.

Being Bold Enables You to Say No

Many women have over the years learnt how to be people pleaser by saying yes to everything, even the things which they are uncomfortable with. People have a funny way of taking you down the road of a guilt trip when you say no to them. Especially if you who have children then you will understand the pressure women feel when their child says with that wounded look "you never do such and such a thing for me". Even when you know it is a big exaggeration something in us as women still just feels bad that they think of us that way. Friends do the same thing and ultimately, people bulk and grant the request even when they know they have just been effectively manipulated.

Some partners are very skilled at this type of manipulation especially when women say no to their sexual overtures. They start by implying that something must be wrong with the woman, they infer that she is frigid, making excuses or some men even claim that she is afraid or they quote some big religious verse. This one usually works on many women because they give in to try and prove they are okay.

Women have to come to a place where they are comfortable saying no. Be bold enough to say what you don't like, say what hurts or upset you. You'll find your mind freer to focus on more productive things rather than be a breeding ground for resentment.

Being Bold Enables You to Say Yes

In the same vein, women have to come to a point where they are comfortable saying yes to themselves. Every time you say yes to things you don't want to you have again said no to your instincts, you have said no to your intuitions, to your needs and to your person. Many women take the proverb love your neighbour as yourself, to extreme heights and they misinterpret the command. Read it again, it says love your neighbour *as* not more than, as you love yourself. Remember practice kindness to yourself first. A stressor of women's lives is the

Don't live by double standards a life of pleasing others

prevalence of double standard and double life leading to a thug of war where on the one hand they are living a life where they are focused on people pleasing and their priorities are misplaced and the struggle to mute their own needs and inclinations.

For that woman who wants a new job you have to be bold enough to put in that application, make that phone call and give your details. You never can tell you might just get the job but you'll never know unless you try. There is a popular saying that all that glitters is not gold, an old friend of mine had a really good comeback, she said "yes it could be diamond" which is even better than gold. Her argument was that she will check out every opportunity to see if it her diamond! You will however never know until you try and if you let fear stop you from trying then it has won. You lose every time you let that inner voice stop you. It's time for you to truly know that you can do it. You can get up and tell yourself "I Can" keep telling yourself until you know it inside of yourself because it is true. Remember you are not saying it to make it true, no . . . no . . . no, you are saying it because it is true, it is your truth. You chose what you believe, its either a half full glass or a half empty glass, both positions are facts, but one is laced with positive energy the other is full of negative energy.

Fear and its Impact on Women's Sex Life

Sex is one of those things people are curious about but no one wants to talk about it! It was not a subject publicly discussed by women of decent circles, it was a completely no go topic for women of certain class and it was definitely unacceptable in Christian circles. Even more tabooed is any talk that sexual relationship in marriage is supposed to be enjoyable for women. Women have routinely seen sex as a duty they have to perform and as such many of them have no expectation of pleasure. They have accepted having crappy sex life's resulting in many women pretending to have fun and feigning orgasm. It has also meant women allowing themselves to be touched in unpleasant ways because of the fear of displeasing their partner.

Whatever you allow people to do to you is an indication of the value you have placed on yourself. Though the intensions of many women is good and can even be seen as laudable, suppression never ever works because suppressing a problem doesn't make it go away. Women have been made to see sexual intercourse with their partners as a one way street where he wants and he comes and takes. They go into the relationship not expecting or desiring any pleasure for themselves. They see it as a duty they have to perform. Suppressing your own needs ultimately leads to resentment, bitterness and anger. It exposes the woman to being hurt because women don't live a compartmentalized life where their emotions are separated out. It flows from the bedroom to the kitchen. Their emotions impact all aspects of their life. So suppressing your desires and needs come out in other areas of your life. If you hurt, abuse or even put yourself down then you are indirectly saying to others that it is okay for them to hurt, abuse and put you down. You are sending them the message that it is okay for them to use you for their personal gratification.

Communication in relationship is the key, talk about your sex life and your sexual needs. You do it enough so you must find ways to talk about what excites you, how you like to be touched and even where you like to be touched. Don't blush! I mean there are women who have been in sexual relationships for over twenty years and have never had an orgasm! Our mothers were different, they didn't know much (I think), they were not exposed to much, they were not even allowed to desire much so many of them were satisfied with that kind of life. With this generation it is very different as people are very exposed and the younger generations are even more so. You see what is happening in the society where extramarital affairs and infidelity is rife among the poor and rich, stars, footballers, the list is endless. Don't suppress yourself, don't suppress your needs. Talk about what is not working with your spouse before you end up in the divorce court or frustration shows its ugly head as an affair. Seek help and talk to each other but act now! Leave the false modesty and shyness behind.

It might be difficult and even embarrassing but the reward makes it worthwhile. Start by telling your partner what you don't like, tell him how you like to be touched, where you like to be touched and even when, talk about what excites you, take that risk. Making love or having sex with your spouse is supposed to be fun for you as well not a duty or a chore. It can only be if you

Making love with your spouse is supposed to be fun not a chore/duty

take ownership and responsibility for how the process goes and you become an active participant. I mean if you let the driver drive your car recklessly or the way he wants (because that's how he knows how to drive) then you can't complain if he revs the engine and spoils the car, speak up!!!

One of the challenges is that many couples have actually stopped being friends so they find it difficult to share little nothings or pleasantries with each other. Their relationships have been reduced to two ships sailing past each other where they talk at each other instead of to each other. Women cannot make love and allow a prolonged exploration of their body from someone she cannot rub minds with on whatever her level is. A woman's body and her mind are intrinsically linked and they take their cue from each other.

For many years, the internalized picture of what a good woman and a good wife should be put a lot of pressure on women to the point many think that pleasure from sex is a bonus—who told you that! Even the good book says that you shall be satisfied from your own cistern$_{10}$. This was from Solomon a man who had over three hundred wives and girlfriends so he must have known what he was talking about. The human body is wired for pleasure so the fun where there is friendship in a relationship is to learn what

Sexual relationship is best when it is enjoyed by both partners

brings pleasure to the other. It should not be produced under a macho demand for sex as a duty, rather a sharing of something valuable and an expression of love. Maybe that's why it is called lovemaking . . .

The vast majority of women are reluctant to talk about their sexual needs with their spouse and they are even more reluctant to initiate sex. Some women are afraid of being seen as a slapper or being seen as pushy or of loose morals. However sexual intercourse is best when it is enjoyed by both parties involved. It's not just about one person's needs, yours matter as well. Encourage your partner to experiment on different parts of your body and tell him what feels good. No one knows what you like or what is best for you as much as yourself. Don't let fear steal from you. An unforgettable woman is bold and boldness will help you defeat and kick fear out of your life. It's time to start living.

Principles for Living

- Boldness is not the absence of fear
- Fear is fuelled by pictures formed in the mind and the pictures people carry in their head
- You cannot grow bigger than the limitations you entertain
- Challenging your thoughts and questioning the taken for granted truths breaks the power of fear
- Thoughts are like seed to a farmer on a well-nourished land
- Whoever assigns and defines your box controls you
- There are three types of people, those within the box, those carrying the box and those who completely destroy the box.
- You are the number one authority in your life so take responsibility for how it is.
- Love others as you love yourself, so first you have to have self-love
- Don't permit others to abuse you.
- Being bold is different from being aggressive
- Don't start a relationship with someone who arouses feelings of fear in you
- Being bold enables you even in the face of fear to do the very thing you fear.
- Failure is not a person it is an event
- If you don't think you will stink so start by getting rid of stinking thinking
- Relationships should be love motivated not fear driven

Five

Spicing up your life

An Unforgettable Woman Takes the Initiative

So many people are wiser after an event or after something have happened. In fact we are smarter in knowing what other people should do. However, the world celebrates and pays those who can think up creative ways of doing things. It celebrates those who can think of it before the need arises not after because it is like administering medication after a person has died. Before the depression starts or before your relationship dies or hits the divorce courts you need to take action and spice up your life and home.

Initiative is the capacity to see what needs to be done and being enterprising enough to do it. It involves taking the first step, leading and having the power to be original or to start a process or venture. Beyond starting, it involves the resources and power to follow through and see something to conclusion. Remember it is not enough to know what to do, it is more important to actually do it₁. Employers want a staff who can work with little or no supervision. In today's economy it is people with initiative who are getting the high paying jobs and the kind of roles that don't result in back ache. You will have to either work with your brain or brawn and unless one is into sports like wrestling working with your

It is not enough to know what to do, it is more important to actually do it₁

brawn will leave you as a low earner. Those with initiative end up as leaders and becoming the managing directors and presidents of big corporations.

Showing initiative is not restricted to high fliers only. It is necessary for the stay at home mums, the shop assistant, the teacher, accounts manager or whatever the profession or life role. Anyone who desires to rise to the top in any sphere has to show a lot of initiative. It is an absolutely necessary quality to have to live as an unforgettable woman. Everyone assumes they know how to be human yet people have to go to college for five to six years to become doctors and four years to be nurses. Yet women are automatically expected to know how to be all these different roles of mother, sister, daughter, friend, woman and even wife. People are learning ***Innovation*** from dysfunctional relationships how to have ***is key to*** good relationships, women are learning from the ***progress and*** unhappy parenting they experienced themselves ***longevity.*** how to be good mothers leading to a long list of dysfunctions passing down the line. As an unforgettable woman, you can start a new line by being innovative in your home, community, relationship and work. You can model for the younger ones coming after you.

Initiative at Home

What do you want to be . . . a mother, a wife? Think about it that's one area where you need to take the initiative. No one teaches you how to be a mother or a wife. Women do a lot of self-education, from friends, their parent's relationships and TV soaps etc. As a parent you need to show initiative at home in the types of meals you prepare, what you cook and how you mix different ingredients together. You need to be innovative in how you answer the children's questions or allow them to help you with the cooking while they are actually making more mess! In fact at home is the one place where you need buckets full of innovation.

Women in their role as mother or wife need to make it easy for others especially their kids to love and admire them. It might be difficult juggling being a mum, driver, cleaner, laundry woman and bread winner for some who are also working mums. No matter how difficult women's lives become, children should not be made to pay for the stressed life of their parents. The sad thing is that they are the ones who get shouted at, bossed around and treated like pest because they want to spend an hour with their mum. They are easily accused of being over demanding, needy and inconsiderate. It is important that women strive to spend quality time with their children rather than quantity time. Make the time you spend with them count and rather than doing things *for them* learn to do things *with them*. What has worked for me so far is that I keep working on ways of being part of the things my kid's call cool.

It is important that women stop doing things for their kids and learn how to do things with them. It brings a different dimension to your relationship and time spent with the children. You can use initiative in organizing the family summer holidays or weekly outings that will involve and satisfy everyone. Think about it, the possibilities are endless. You can be creative, innovative and show initiative, it is the stuff unforgettable women are made of.

Initiative in Relationships

You can show initiative when you are dating or when your relationship seems to be boring and getting in a rut. As it is popularly said, familiarity breeds contempt so how can you make a familiar relationship become unfamiliar again. How can you restore some excitement in being with each other? You can order a meal and create a romantic atmosphere at home, or make a dinner booking and call your partner up at work asking him to meet you for dinner. Do the unusual, change things around. Relationships after children become just about the kids. Get a life and don't keep using your children as ice breakers! Some use discussion about their kids as conversation interjections or stimulators. Try spending thirty minutes every day talking to each about how your day went, what you saw on your way out, just little nothings about your day and you will develop friendship after a while.

Have what I call your 'Me' time as that can help reduce your stress levels, have some girlie time with your mates. If you are attracted to someone, take the bull by the horn and say hello, if they are single then go for it. After all trying never kills. The worse outcome is being told no and I promise you it can't kill you. Spice up your relationship. After the kids have gone to bed then a bit of sheer lace might do the trick but first it is important that you actually have a real relationship with your spouse where you see and know each other again if not it will just be another act.

Initiative at work

No matter what area you want to work in either as a career woman or a family woman, there is room for initiative. Do your work effectively and make contributions as the need arises. Come up with creative ways that can improve the quality of your work. Unless you are a factory worker or in line production where you have to do things the same way, you need to constantly be evaluating the quality of your service and keep looking at innovative ways of increasing your value. If you only do what you are paid for then you are easily replaceable. If on the other hand, you give more than you are worth then your employers know that they will need more than they are presently paying you to replace your role. Think of ways to increase your value.

If you only do what you are paid for then you are easily replaceable

If we consider the woman from our story, she wanted to meet the dinner guest and do something special for him. She initiated the meeting, she wasn't sent, she wasn't pressured into doing it neither did she do it to please others. It was her personal choice, she must have thought about it, asked herself all kinds of question until she came up with the idea. In her mind, she must have thought through the various possibilities, obstacle and all that could go wrong. Her focus was on another person, what she could do to make his life easier.

Engaging the thinking process plays a big role to showing initiative. The major difficulty is that most people allow their brains lethargy when it comes to important things. Many women and men as well but more women invest more of their thinking power on what is not working rather than asking themselves "how" can I change this . . ., how can I be . . ., how do I . . . Every time we ask the question how, it draws an answer because it creates an expectant heart. Some women would rather spend their time thinking unproductive thoughts which leads to depression and sleepless nights and they end up making money for doctors and counsellors. One reason this remains problematic is that many women become experts at majoring on the minor and they minor on the major things. To be able to take the initiative, you will need the following helpers.

- *Sensitivity to the needs of others*
- *Be wise about where you pour your affection so you don't waste it!*
- *Think of others and their need*
- *A good understanding of problems and situations*
- *Be able to look ahead and see a need before you get there*
- *Question or challenge situations*
- *Ask the how and not the why question*

Remember, life will only pay you what you are worth and so some people's time gets more monetary reward than others. It will pay you based on what you give to it, what you put into it. In fact, some people's time gets €8.74 per hour while some get €1,000 for an hours work. Some people are very self-righteous and they think it is a bad thing to have money. Many erroneously misquote the bible however it says "money is a defense",$_3$, it is really important to get the principles right because there are more women in the Christian church than there are men. It is the love of money that is not good$_1$ The thing with money is that it takes on the character of whoever holds it. If a wicked person holds money he will use it for wicked ends, to control, abuse and have his own way. If a generous and compassionate person *Money takes on the character of its owner* has money, they will see people's needs and help them even before being asked.

What makes the difference? I will leave this with you as food for thought. What needs are you meeting, whose needs are you meeting, how are you meeting those needs, what would you like to achieve, how can you get it, what do you need to do, for how long and what is the benefit. The first rule for economic success is about meeting the needs of others and the more needs you meet, the more economically successful you will be. The more needs you meet, the more unforgettable you will be but your motive must always be right. You can read about motive as a desirable quality in women in later chapters.

I can just imagine the woman from our story pondering over what she could do. She would have asked questions like—what is his need now, what is he going through and what would he like. Many women decide to only meet the needs within their home and that is a great thing to do but that is your reward. The best you can get is probably social welfare and they have calculated the payment so much that you can never have more than enough on social welfare payments. Remember, promotion comes from above. One interpretation of this is that only those above you can promote you. Those economically lower than you can connect you to people who can promote you, they can even recommend you and at best they can celebrate you but real promotion and increase comes from those above where you are. Make sure your innovation is bigger than you. Celebrate the great connections that have come around you.

If we take for example, mobile phones, why do you think they are still selling and making so much money? It is because as you save up and buy the latest model of phones, the manufacturers add one more innovation to that model and immediately yours becomes an old model and you or another set of people start aspiring and saving up for it. What about television, first it was black and white, then they had coloured tubes now it is the size, wide screen or super wide, then flat screen and then really flat, now we have HD, 3D, and smart TV's. I mean the innovation seems endless and that is what adds value to the technology.

In your life learn how to spice up your atmosphere. I don't mean with drugs or alcohol that comes to destroy you! I mean value that is in you that no one can take away. Remember real value is the thing that can stand the test of time. So when you use drugs or drinks it only produces great feeling for three hours then it is over. That is not real value is it? It is only an imitation of value and it is only there to taunt you. Real value is about you not things you put in yourself to alter your mood. This type of mood alteration is temporary and it will fade away leaving more sorrow in its wake. Take the initiative, it will make your life more interesting.

Principles for Living

- Money is a defence
- You will have to either work with your brain or brawn
- Always give more than you are worth, it increases your value and makes you hard to replace
- Showing initiative is vital for every role in life
- Strive to spend quality time with your children rather than quantity time
- Money takes on the character of its owner
- You can only be promoted by those above you.

Six

Knowledge opens doors

An Unforgettable Woman is Knowledgeable

Knowledge is power and ignorance many say is a disease. One cannot neglect the importance of knowledge in the human world. In fact, in society today women are not given eminence if they are uninformed. Knowledge helps people make the right decisions and at the same time it illuminates the human mind. One can say that the level of knowledge people have essentially defines who they are, where they can go and what they can be. Again, for emphasis sake *Knowledge is power.*

Benefits of knowledge

Life will pay you what you are worth and that value is based on your contributions, the problems you solve and the solutions you provide. It is influenced by the things you know and their relevance to the world. The world only pays for *Everyone has* what it needs not what entertains you! The role *twenty four* individuals have to play in their destinies, the *hours. Make* height they attain, the feats they accomplish and *yours count!* how they are treated cannot be underestimated. Remember, everyone has twenty four hours, you have to decide what you put into yours. Your job is to make it count!

Information is key to new horizons. We regularly say it, give a man a fish and you feed him for a day, teach a man to fish and you feed him for life. Knowledge and education is that tool by which you can be feed for life. It can boast your confidence and self-esteem, it can open doors and give you back the power and control of your situation.

If we consider the unforgettable woman in our story, she knew the dinner guest was in town, she knew his status, she knew where to find him and that he was at Simon's house. She knew what he looked like if not she could have poured the oil on the wrong person, which she didn't! The scenario showed us a woman who was aware and had the inside scoop on the dignitaries visit. In a word I would say she was very informed and knowledgeable of things happening around her. It was as if an ambassador or a president was in town and she knew about it, she knew about his culture and that he would not reject or misunderstand the idea of perfume being poured on his head. As an unforgettable woman, you have to stay aware and connected.

Some women might go to the extreme and use this as an excuse to be in everyone's business, please know it's not about becoming a busy body or 'nosy parker' sticking ones nose in everyone else's business. Not for gossip or to spread malicious news. It is safer for your peace to mind your business. The more informed you are generally, the more confident you'll feel. You will not appear ignorant which is a word used by some as an insult. It is a state of being unaware or simple as some people have termed it. Good information will get your life out of a rut.

One reason many people still die from cancer is because scientists have not discovered a cure for it. The more they know about what causes it the more they can address it. In the same way, ignorance steals lives and destinies$_3$. There was a time when malaria was a killer disease in Africa but with increased information on the strains, their breeding condition and the atmosphere where they can thrive, malaria is much easier to treat now. There is even some medication people can take once a week for prevention. Think about it, the reason many people are stuck is because of what they don't know. Everyone has things they don't know and in a way it is good as it keeps people searching and motivated. The extreme case of ignorance is what is damaging. Think about it, if you know which company is looking for a staff with the kind of skills you have you will be in employment so fast in fact the social welfare officers will not see you for dust. Ignorance is a limitation and it is the truth that you know that will make you free₄.

To be an unforgettable woman, you have to make it a personal choice to acquire knowledge. Who said you are too old to study, who said you cannot get a degree or a masters. Who really said there was no need to educate women? With the advent of adult education and the lenient conditions for adult learners the opportunities cannot be denied. It is time to get a life woman, have a dream and raise your standards. There are part-time courses women can attend when the kids are in school, evening courses and online options. For those who are not academically inclined, there are practical trainings such as baking, pottery, photography, sculpting etc. try

Education is not a choice but an obligation you owe yourself

your hand at something. Remember an unforgettable woman has knowledge and education is not a choice but an obligation you owe to yourself.

Ignorance is a Disease

When I say ignorance is a disease, I am referring to the type that corrodes the mind and steals destinies. Every attempt must be made to stamp out ignorance especially in the lives of women. In this modern age of technology, people don't even have to leave their homes to acquire knowledge. The level of knowledge available to individuals is dependent on the quality of information in the person's sphere. Information is produced so fast especially through social media that if you update new information into the newsfeed on Facebook in less than one minute, your news will have become old. Ignorance is a sin a person commits against himself. Ignorance should make people uncomfortable but again, many easily excuse themselves.

The knowledge of women has typically been seen as limited in many areas of life. For example people assume that women are not good at maths or maths related jobs, people assume that male drivers are better than female driver's, an endless list of stereotyped roles. Society has for many years dictated the kind of topics women should talk about and be interested in which has in turn conditioned so many women that they actually conform to the dictates and expectations of society and others. It is important though for women not to limit their knowledge to what society says is good women topics or scope.

To expand your circle of influence you need to increase the circle of knowledge. Wisdom they say is the main thing but with wisdom comes the need for understanding$_1$. And they are all interlinked because to gain understanding, you need knowledge. In other words, the more knowledge you have the more understanding you will display.

> ***Ignorance is a sin you commit against yourself***

As an unforgettable woman, it is important to be aware of what is happening around you including the latest technological advancement, politics, prices of gas, the exchange rate, lending rates, unemployment rate, the national budget, wars, natural disaster and so on. The truth is that you don't need to know everything in detail. In fact there are very few people who can boast of being knowledgeable about every subject. Develop yourself and be able to carry on a reasonable conversation, be well versed in subjects that you are interested in, not just gender or stereotyped topics but issues that are relevant to the society that can make a difference to life. Practical sources of knowledge include reading newspapers, journals, listening to the news. It includes knowing when State, national and International events are being staged for example the Olympics, world cup . . . . It doesn't matter that it is sports. Sometimes if you are not interested in knowing it for yourself, you can do it as part of your children's education or to enable you carry on a relaxed conversation with others. Though simple and common knowledge, many women have turned their interests away from such things and many have left it for the men, an action that again reinforces stereotypes.

Don't get left behind

Some women have become skilled and titled as the Managing Director, Chief Executive Officer of the kitchen or the newscaster of the latest fashion or who is sleeping with whom. Some are so versed in the latest update on soaps, reality shows and Mexican movies that one would almost be tempted to give them the role of broadcaster!

Everyone is informed really, the issue is what they decide is necessary knowledge. Indeed women are quite informed and very knowledgeable but the question is how much value does the knowledge many women invest their time in add to society. This causes many women to being relegated to the background. One can notice the role assignment even at parties, the segregation and automatic expectations of some.

Stop being the Managing Director, CEO of the kitchen or the newscaster of the latest fashion and who is sleeping with whom.

Technology is another area many women get easily relegated and left behind. Don't be struggling to type a letter on a typewriter when a computer is light years ahead in abilities. There are all kinds of technological advancement through social media such as blogs, twitter, Facebook. They are not just for teenagers or men. To increase your value, you have to increase what you know,

Principles for living

- You don't have to know it all, you only need to know how to get information.
- There is usually nothing new under the sun. If you have thought of it so have others. Search for what they have done and make it your starting point.
- Stand on others shoulder and start from where they are
- Your connections are important,
- We need people but it is not a permission to be needy
- Don't dismiss things just because you don't understand it
- Choose your connections because the company you keep will make or destroy you
- Knowledge reduces fear
- As knowledge is power, so is ignorance a disease
- Knowledge boast confidence and self-esteem,
- It increases your circle of influence and encourages others to listen and value you
- Your economic value is proportional to the level of knowledge you have.
- All leaders are readers
- Whatever you are reading today is an indication of where you will be in the next five years.

Seven

You don't have to be a boy to make it

An Unforgettable Woman is Caring and Tender

The show of tenderness and femininity in today's society seems to be viewed as a dysfunction and some think it is an invitation to cheat and mistreat people with such qualities. The unforgettable woman at that dinner was not afraid or shy about revealing and using her feminine side that day. We can deduce that from her actions if we consider how carefully she must have carried the box to where the dinner guest was seated. She didn't fall, though everyone was watching and castigating her. She didn't drop the box out of being nervous neither did she spill the perfume when she broke the box. Even the pieces of the broken box did not cut through her hand neither did it hurt the dinner guest. It takes a level of carefulness and tenderness to be able to accomplish this in adverse conditions without an accident. To be an unforgettable woman you need this tender and caring attitude for people and life generally. An unforgettable woman cannot do without it.

Being caring and tender is one of the original attributes of women or I should say a feminine quality which is fast fading from society. People who are tender are actually considered as too soft and some see it as an undesirable trait. However, being caring and tender is vital for humanity to function effectively because it is what helps us to love, care and be sensitive to each other.

You are great just as you are

Society doesn't make it easy for women and even men to show their tender sides as some people have been abused and taken for granted as a result. It is however important to be aware of the lines which can easily become blurred such that people cross them unthinkingly. The grounds gained on behalf of women by feminist and equality movements who have championed the rights of women cannot be overstated as they have made it possible for women to vote, work in any sector they desire, rise to management levels and generally have equal rights to be treated well. Though there still seems to be a lot more to be done we have to acknowledge their efforts and accomplishments. In seeking to liberate and build women up, the challenge in our society full of people

Women should not have to behave like men to be accepted in professionalcircles neither should they take on male attributes to be treated equally.

who go from one extreme to the other is how to maintain the balance and not end up with women who want to be men. The purpose of the equality struggle by women is not for women to be like men but to be treated equally and have equal access. It is to have a society of women who have a healthy self-esteem, who can stand in their place and don't need to wear masculine or dull coloured clothes to fit into a man's 'environment', job, clubs or games. It is about women who should not have to behave like men to be accepted in professional circles or feel pressured to take on male attributes just to fit in or be treated equally.

It is vital that society understands that men and women are wired differently for their purpose. Beyoncé sang "if I were a boy . . ." but you know what, we are not boys and how we thank God that women are not boys! What kind of world would we have! (Sorry I couldn't resist the dig). Seriously though, women have great attributes and qualities that should be developed in themselves and in their daughters. Women should celebrate the stuff they are made of and not be busy wishing them away. You are great just as you are and you don't need to be like another to succeed, make it or be happy. A friend of my sisters told her husband that if was possible for them to come back to life again that she will come back as a man and make sure her now husband came back to life as a woman. The joy she was going to have from it was to marry him and have the pleasure of treating him exactly how he treats her! I wonder if this was possible will it be seen as a promise or a threat to the male population of this generation.

Men and women are different and they get treated differently where in many instances males are more advantageously treated than females. Rather than turning women into men or escalating the antagonism, resentment and competition between both sexes, the lines of differential treatment between them needs to be decreased. We can begin to see males and females as equal but different with each serving complementary purposes. One way I like to describe this difference between them is if we consider them as a truck and a Porsche. Both of them are automobiles, they have engines, they run on fuel and are modes of transport, yet one is small and the other is gigantic. In spite of their differences and similarities, they are powerful, valuable and imposing in very different ways and for very different reasons. Now I won't call it and say which one is a metaphor for males and which is for females but you can email me your thoughts.

It is time for society to begin to show true value and respect for women by taking off the invisible limitation and barriers around women's lives. If we adapt Martin Luther king's ideology then women need to be judged based on their ability rather than their gender, tone of voice, the expectations of others, traditions and customs of men, shape of their shoulders or the size of their chest! Women need to be encouraged to be themselves. Hopefully we can have confident female chief executives who can boldly go to board meetings in a hot pink suit if that is what she fancies and not get treated like a floozy!

Women don't have to behave or become like men to be heard, employed, earn the same salary or to have a good relationship. So maybe rather than saying act like a woman and think like a man as some books and songs claim, women need to just stop at *think*. Think like you, think like a woman in her full elements. Don't think like a woman programmed by society full of limitations and stereotypes. Honestly, you don't need to become a player or user to become successful. There is a song that says don't get even get out! So as a woman you can develop yourself and still be feminine. Women don't have to dress like men, talk like men or be hard and unfeeling just to prove that they are okay or just as good. It is important to know that most men are not looking for a hard woman. They need your female tenderness not stupidity to complement the way they are. Please ladies *tenderness is not synonymous with stupidity.*

What people need from us as women is tenderness and it should not be mistaken for stupidity. The design of an object gives an indication of how they function, the same with human beings so if you see the shoulder set of men, it is square, hard and for many their shoulders look unyielding while that of women is soft and naturally rounded except of cause those who have gone to build their muscles and lift weight.

Tenderness is not synonymous with stupidity.

It is not easy to be a high-flying executive and still be tender and soft, yet it is not impossible. You can be all that you have to be to get the job done but you don't have to become tough and uncaring to make tough decisions. It is not duplicity, it is just one of the many qualities that you have as a woman. The same way you can be a daughter one-minute, then a wife at the same time then a little child walks into the room and instantly you are a mother . . . Daughter, Wife and Mother, all in one person and all present at the same time.

Independent and strong women—pros and cons

Women are expected to be the warmer and the more subservient sex but with societal advancement, more women are growing independent and fending for themselves. Also, with the increasing economic crisis, traditional roles assigned to both genders are changing and families are more flexible about who is the bread winner. In fact more families seem to have no choice as that decision is taken out of their hands and is dictated by who has a paying job. Thankfully, the days when women were confined to home and kitchen duties—barefoot and pregnant, in public attitude seems to be gone but you'll be amazed how many women are still held in such roles. However, the number of women who are educated or can access education has been on the increase. We also have more enterprising and employed women which has to a great extent impacted on making more women independent.

The capability of women to earn gives them more freedom as they can provide their own accommodation, clothes, food, entertainment and even gadgets for those who like such things. One of the difficulties encountered by Independent, strong and confident high flying women is that they have gotten very used to being in control of their own lives. They are used to taking care of themselves and their own needs that it can be a huge challenge if they have to rely on someone who is not as dynamic as themselves. Many hardworking women before they entered into relationship have gotten into the habit of fending for themselves, paying their own bills, planning their own holidays without consulting another person. They work hard and for long hours, carry their own heavy shopping, they service and fix their cars at the garage on their own and even change their car tyres and engine oil themselves!

The hard part is learning how to balance it when Miss independent meets Mr indecisive or Mr Available! Whoever you settle for ladies, remember if you were Miss Independent at the start of the relationship who insisted on doing everything by herself and for herself, ten years into the relationship you cannot blame your partner for not doing those same things you insisted you didn't need a man to do for you. The root of such problems is that people change or they want to change. After the relationship has blossomed and they are settled and the games stage ended they want more and they change. Ultimately, women end up complaining feeling dissatisfied because they end up in a relationship where it seems they are the only ones doing everything. This is a very common reason for many relationship break ups and why many women end up resenting their partners.

Ladies! Ladies!! Ladies!!! You must know that whatever you do to start a relationship you have to keep doing it to maintain the relationship. Save yourself some stress and know this, it is really difficult to change the terms of the contract midway. If you enticed your partners by showing him that you are strong and independent, you will have to keep being that way to maintain the relationship. What will happen is that you will attract men *Don't get your partner hooked on "super woman" you who can do everything. It is very hard to shake* who need strong independent woman because in relationships people gravitate towards what they don't have. It is the law of opposites attract. Women however easily forget the beginning of the relationship where they tried to prove they are independent, strong women. Don't get me wrong there is absolutely nothing wrong with being strong and independent in fact everything is right with it. However if you get your partner hooked on the idea of you that is a *"super woman"* who can do everything it is very hard to shake. Don't take on more than you really want to and don't try and prove a lifestyle you won't want to have in five years' time. I love the African proverb that encapsulates the point I have used so many words to explain. It says "what you will not take as rich women don't take it as a poor woman".

Emergency kit for Women

Talking about women becoming super woman reminds me of when I had my second child. I was running around trying to be everything to everyone, care for my two kids, the home, the church and its members, going to school full time, working twenty hours part time and completing one hundred hours of one on one Counselling client hours for my Counselling qualification. At one point, I was exhausted and ready to drop—oh and did I and to that list hours and hours of unpaid phone Counselling for friends. One day I just told myself look slow down, if you drop down dead today all these people will survive. In fact give it six months, one nice looking gal will appear to sympathize with my husband and help him take care of my wonderful children. She will be presented with a readymade family without even having to endure the nine months of being bloated with oily face, back pain and feeling extended on every side. She won't even have endured the pain of going through labour. All for what I asked myself . . . I had to decide what was important and urgent, what could wait and what the priority at that time of my life was. That period was another turning point in my life (I have many of such points!). It was when I realized I am number one priority in my own life. It's like the air hostesses instruction about the gas mask in case of emergency. They always advice passengers to use the mask first then use it for your dependents. I had to do a check in my

You are number one priority in your life because you can only give what you have

life and I decided to look for things people could help me with and as we Irish are very fond of saying "mind yourself" became my personal watchword to me. Today I give you that same gift, *'mind yourself'*.

What I am saying is that some women are doing a lot of things and usually what happens is they give up their lives and dreams for others. Twenty years down the line when the kids are married or away in school all that is usually left is a heart full of unfulfilled dreams. Many call this feeling or this phase the empty nest syndrome. At the end of the day, some women end up frustrating their children, friends or even family because they want to continue to live through them. The dilemma is that these people who you love dearly no longer need you or are no longer kids but are fully grown and are even parents with families of their own. So some women's continued good intentioned but unsolicited support and advice begins to be seen as overbearing, controlling, interfering and whatever else they can come up with.

If you short change yourself and live a life without a personal dream and vision, you have only yourself to blame when everything is gone. Hold on to your dream woman! Find a balance and make it work. If your dream is to mind the kids then do it with a glad heart and tenderly, not hard and complaining. Do it as a conscious decision not because you feel you had no choice. Again I say don't complain about what you permit. Start making choices you can enjoy.

> ***Don't short change yourself by living a life without a personal dream and vision***

Mind reading doesn't work in relationships

Women who are most likely to be susceptible are those in relationship with insecure or weaker people, especially those who are not ambitious, strong or motivated who constantly need someone to *mummy* them. Some women have taken the idea of being a mother to all new heights especially African women who are constantly told to take their husband as their first son. That argument makes it okay for the woman to have to do everything including all the cooking, cleaning, serving and being the provider of their pleasure!

Mummy me type men are those who need a woman to remind them to get up and go to work, they need a woman to remind them to apply for more than one job a day. The type who waits for the woman to fix the electric bulb when it blows a fuse or the common one is those who will wait till the woman comes home before they can eat. Not because they are waiting to share quality time with her and to enjoy the woman's company . . . no . . . no . . . no rather it's because they have decided that it is the woman's duty to make the meals and as such they cannot cook.

One cannot really blame men who present as '*mummy me*' type because women's traditional role enables them and by so doing disable these men. You are not doing your partner any favours neither are you helping your kids because you are the mirror that reflects to them how to be human. We hear talks from women about their partners who cannot make their own bed or such other things. Hello!!! Such women take on the typical super woman role and later become the Martyr. The truth is that everyone is responsible for the choices they make. It is your life and so if you don't like it change it, if you don't want to change it then don't complain about it. A lot of women's lives

You are the mirror that reflects to the younger ones how to be human.

have been compromised because they are expected to maintain a sense of humility because that is the "proper" way to be as women, They silently hope that their partners can get it that they are not happy with the way things are. Please know that your partner, colleague, boss, manager or friend is not a mind reader. That obnoxious colleague at work is not a mind reader and in fact, it suites them to pretend they don't know or cannot see the effect their actions are having on you. You need to open your mouth and speak because many times silence can erroneously be taken as consent.

Don't become a freak of nature

If you find yourself in any of the scenarios above or similar stress inducing situation, try and be wise. Remember, a wise woman builds her home but a foolish one with her own hands pulls it down$_1$. If you are the higher earner at home or should I say the boss and you are doing everything, or you live alone and fend for yourself, the natural tendency is to become harder by trying to be the male and female at the same time. This is particularly prevalent with single parenting. However, that is not the way the human has been designed to function, it makes you into a freak to be both male and female at the same time. Please don't try and be both. It's so easy to take on the role and the persona as it becomes a coping mechanism that helps many handle the changes and unnatural demands being placed on them. An unforgettable woman is first a woman so please maintain your feminine side.

Be yourself and do the job as best as you can. Please remember you are a woman so consciously cultivate the tenderness in you. You will be remembered for that tenderness that is why it is easier for a woman to cry, get emotional, fall in love and yes even get hurt. Women, need to remain tender because it is a core part of our nature. Consider female voices, touch, handshake and even the bones are all more tender than the males. Please understand that women are tender, not weaker, not stupid and definitely not of less importance just more tender. Women can acknowledge and accept that tenderness because it can make a difference. Envision the left and right hand, both are hands but they function differently, complementing each other. Remember, tenderness is a core part of an *Unforgettable Woman* so stay tender.

Principles for Living

- Tenderness is not synonymous with weaker, stupid or less important
- Trying to be both man and woman will make you into a freak of nature
- You can never appreciate your femininity unless you will be happy being a woman if you had a choice
- As a woman you have a right to be happy.
- Men and women are like Porsche and a Truck, they are powerful, valuable and imposing but in very different ways
- Tenderness softens a woman's outlook and enables her to see the societies needs
- Tenderness is not synonymous with stupidity
- What you do to start a relationship you have to continue doing it to maintain that relationship.
- People become more of what they are so be careful of the things you think will go away or change with time!
- An Irish gift to you—*Mind yourself*
- You are the number one priority in your life
- Cater for yourself because the stronger you are the more you have to give

Eight

Modest but Stylish

"Fashion can be bought, Style one must possess"
Edna Woolman Chase

An Unforgettable Woman is Stylish

It is all too easy for many women to take themselves out of the category of stylish people. However, being stylish does not mean being a fanatical follower of fashion rather it is an expression of a person's individuality. It helps to reveal a person's character, mood and even their dreams. A stylish woman is one that dresses for herself rather than trying to please others. When it comes to amazing, audacious style, individuality and personal panache plays a big part. Giving ones inner style queen a little bit of room to breathe you'll be amazed how much creativity is within each woman.

The woman from our story did not use a substandard container or just any old box, she used an alabaster box which in her time was unusual and special. The perfume itself was not just some cheap mixture rather it was quite expensive and of very good quality. When she broke the box, the aroma filled the whole room and perfumed the atmosphere. The text actually described it as a precious perfume and if this woman's story had occurred in the times we are in now the perfume will definitely have been a designer label. Seriously though, as an unforgettable woman, it is important for you to have good taste. It totally enabled her to change the atmosphere in that meeting.

Your individual style will determine the atmosphere in your home. If as a woman you are chic, controlled, cheerful, stylish or even disorganized your home will reflect the way you are. Even the atmosphere and the dynamics in women's homes will mirror the kind of people they are. The traces of you will be visible all over the place. Even the absence of one's personality and touch in their home is an indication of that person's position there. It could mean the person is not consulted in her home. It could also reflect that the woman doesn't have a voice in her relationship. For some it could be an indication that she trusts other people's opinion over her own. The same deductions and interpretations can be made if the woman is loud, opinionated, controlling, a smoker, a drinker and different other ways women can be. Your style will ultimately determine the atmosphere in your home, place of work and family.

A stylish woman is one that dresses for her own enjoyment rather than to please others

Without judging your lifestyle, many women feel helpless and some are even oblivious of the implications of living a life where style is relegated to the background. Some wonder what they can do to address the situation in their homes. The purpose of highlighting these qualities is to enable women see their role in the kind of life they live. It is to give women pointers of how they can change things around especially for those who are dissatisfied with where they are. It is to give women options that will enable them make informed decisions. So really not everyone can relate to becoming unforgettable, however, my hope is that women who are tired of their present position and are looking for change will find something in this book that will lead you to live a more fulfilled life. A life where women begin to make conscious choice as it is all too easy to pass the buck to the next person and abdicate oneself from all responsibilities, a process which never really works anyway.

True change comes first with an awareness of the situation and then taking responsibility for one's part in it. Women can take their power back by shifting from being the victim in whatever situation it may be. Don't get me wrong people might have grievously harmed you but you get nothing from positioning yourself as the victim. The victim mould is really weak and disempowering. It is a position that says "there is nothing I can do". There is always something people can do. There might be risks involved so plan carefully but you can always do something about your situation. Not taking action is an action in itself and not making a decision is a decision. Remember it is not just the things that happened that mar a life it is how people respond to those things that happened. The man who fails is not the one who gets knocked down it is the person who can't get back up.

> *"Not taking action is an action itself and not making a decision is a decision itself"*

Tobacco and smoke styled homes

The heavy smoker who is addicted to smoking and can't seem to kick the habit might start from the implications of her continued actions or rather inaction. That woman will need to consciously decide that she loves smoking so much she doesn't mind that every item coming out of her house smells of stale cigarette! She must quit expecting her friends to tip toe around her pretending they cannot smell everything she gives them or that they are not choking from the natural stale cigarette cologne coming from her. Some women are more skilled at suppressing the smell of tobacco I must say. An addiction to smoking is another way of saying the individual loves the 'benefits' attached to the problem (this time smoking) so much that they are not prepared to do the *hard work* involved in effecting a change. When faced with opposing situation, the natural tendency is to choose the easier of the two options. In other words, people gravitate to the option they associate with less pain. The downside of this is that the easier pain is not always the best choice!

The medical model of what sickness is has given so many people a crotch and escape route for all forms of human wilful behaviours. Some researchers are even looking for genes that make some people more susceptible to alcohol. Some are looking for genes that make people more susceptible to eating to the point that they are so obese they have to be stretchered out of their homes! What is happening is that many people have become too lenient with themselves whereby they very readily say yes to their every need and impulse. Think about the last time you realized you were two sizes bigger than you were six months ago, it usually involves a certain level of rationalization. People excuse and excuse themselves till the situation becomes a problem. When did you go from a size ten when you got married to a size twelve and now you are a size twenty! Learn to say no to those unhealthy bodily desires. Today is your first step towards controlling the things you have hitherto allowed to control you before now.

The Alcohol styled home

The person addicted to alcohol or as some like to minimize the problem and call it heavy or social drinker or the woman who regularly has one too many also creates an unsafe environment for others, for herself and her dependents. If you are involved, whatever it is called, that woman needs to consciously decide that she doesn't mind that her children have to time their visits to the neighbour's house three times a day pretending to visit just so they can get their meals as their mum or parents would rather spend all the families resources and income stocking the cupboards with drink or drugs. It is much easier to blame it on addiction, what people did to you years ago, the rape, abusive relationship or whatever other upheaval has been either in your past or sadly for some is still on going. It is a very difficult situation to be, I have counselled enough people to know that. But just like the merry go round, someone has to stop it if not it remains a continuous vicious circle. Someone needs to break the circle and the way life is you have to decide you've had enough and get off the merry go round.

Children have no return policy neither do they have a one week no obligation trial.

Unfortunately, many people become so depressed and resort to alcohol which in itself has no answer and their kids for those who are parents get exposed to the very same risky and abusive environment they endured growing up. Such families expose the children to exactly the same type of abuse they experienced at the hands of strangers, abusers within their own homes or whatever else is out there. Every mother has a responsibility to her children and they are not supposed to become state property! Every child has the right to be safe—Child first is the policy so take care of the children you bring into the world. Having children is hard but it can be quite rewarding. However, people should not have children if they are not ready to take care of them. Unfortunately children have no return policy neither do they have a one week no obligation trial. You can't just give them back and get your figure or your life back. So know before you do!

Seeking help

Some women make it so difficult for their kids, spouse and friends to admire them. Everywoman knows how hard life can be and has been trying to juggle being a wife, mother, driver, cook and everything else in between. So the expectation of many women is that those around them should be grateful for the service they provide because of the hard work associated with the roles and responsibilities they are lumbered with. However hard that life is, we cannot carry the weight of that hardness on our person as women. No matter how stressed out a woman is, it does not mean she should pick up her children from school looking obviously like someone who has not had a shower or who doesn't work! Many kids are appreciative and excited that their mums or parents come to pick them from school but you should also hear the pride in their voice as they speak about what their mum does. It's about balance ladies. The stay at home mum and the working mum both have payoffs so maximize the strength in your position. Don't make your kids want to hide when you go to pick them up from school. Showing your admirable side should not be once a week, when you are going to parties, church or social outings. An unforgettable woman has to be stylish and represent ***Change is*** herself well in her home and beyond. ***possible***

You probably know the fable of the two men who fell into a hole, one of them decided the hole was too deep and that it was rather unfortunate it happened to him. He then proceeds to sit in that hole and be buried there. A second person who met the same fate cried a little and began to look around for things he could use to climb his way out of the hole. Seek help if you can't help yourself. Talk to people who are in a position to help and share the problem, as the popular saying goes, a problem shared is a problem half solved. I don't know if that is completely true but at least it works for AA because the first thing they do is share the problem. Remember change is possible. The way you are today is not the way you were twenty years ago. So if you could change from there to how you are now then you can change again to how you want to be. You got damaged by something that happened to you then it can also be fixed even if it is a ten, twenty or a hundred per cent repair. Let's go for it and seek help. Remember your unforgettable moments begin with each move you make.

Living a dynamic Life

Many women have been known to lose their partners to younger girls or maybe I should say other girls. No matter the reason, it is not a good experience to have and it is difficult to handle. At the same time though it is important that women should not be the ones encouraging or blowing the fans of trouble in their relationship. Life is dynamic and circumstances are constantly changing. So to be unforgettable, women have to keep improving. You cannot remain the same way you were ten years ago—"the same today, now and forever". Only God has that quality! Some women who have been in long term relationships find that the person they got married to ten years ago has changed and the woman still remains the same. Relationships that started since high school where as a young couple they needed to skimp and save every penny and now the many years of hard work and extensive education have paid off such that their spouse or partner has moved on. He now wears designer labels, good leather shoes and he would even wear a well cut suit when the occasion warrants.

. . . The woman still cringes at the thought of spending a few euros to get a good cleanser for her face. Some women refuse to groom their hair not to mention their nails and the usual excuse is that the nails will be broken in a day with all the cooking and cleaning she needs to do. You know what, let them break! At least have the pleasure of having groomed nails or hair for the twenty four hours that you can. You need to know this; no one will treat you better than you treat yourself if you go out with your spouse or date dressed like his mother! If you portray an image that says look at me "I am trash, I am not worth it" that is exactly how you will be treated. You expose yourself to the risk of getting looks that say you are nothing. Someone once said that "people will address you the way you are dressed". Remember it is not an absolute one hundred per cent but ninety nine out of a hundred says it is true. It's not a matter of swinging from one extreme to the other. Women don't have to go from having an "I don't care" attitude to becoming vain caring only about her outward appearance. Balance my friends . . . a balanced attitude to your appearance is a good place to start.

Being stylish is not about women running after every new fashion or wearing killer heels they can't walk with. It simply means you start taking care of yourself, clean up, and generally lift up your standard. If you slap on just anything available looking as if you were pulled out from under rubble, tell me if you were not you will you be attracted to yourself the way you are now. . Many people demand and expect to be shown respect but if a person shows disrespect and disregard for their own bodies by not being able to wash and dress it decently, why should anyone else respect that person. Respect is earned, not just by some but it should be by all of us, if not we cannot complain about what we get or however we get treated. You have to play your part. Please women value and respect yourself! The way you style yourself is an indication of the value you place on yourself. Dress yourself with dignity because it is the stuff an unforgettable woman is made of. Learn to cultivate an unforgettable style.

Where are you going in life? Who are those at that point in their lives right now? Take a look around you and evaluate yourself to see if you look like where you are going. We have to look like where we are going, so women need to dress the part, talk the part and yes look the part. Don't forget to add the brains for the part whatever the part is. If you want to end up looking like a junkie that is very easy, don't wash yourself or your clothes, roll out of bed and pull on any dirty, old jeans and leave your hair untidy and half the

A woman's style tells a lot about the value she places on herself

job is done! Have you ever seen a nurse who cannot imagine herself in a nurses uniform in the hospital, she will have done herself out of a job. You have the right to choose either to look like a depressed, lonely, unhappy woman with the weight of the whole world on your shoulder. Or you can look like a strong, confident, self-aware woman who can take a licking and keep on ticking. A woman who can handle whatever challenge life throws at her without falling apart or giving up.

I know that life may have given many women some really heavy knocks here and there. I know it only too well, being a woman myself. In fact, most women's lives are full of them but winners are those who have decided not to allow life or happenings keep them down. You too can do the same, face life with a positive attitude. The way you dress and look can greatly affect you attitude. I assure you, if I stayed down every time life gave me a knock you will not be reading this book today. It would have remained a dream in me never a reality.

Work on yourself, improve yourself, go for courses if you must, learn how to read, write whatever you need to increase your economic value. Remember, it's never too late. People find a sort of satisfaction that their life is not so bad by comparing themselves with people in worse situations. The danger there is that it has a tendency to encourage people to continue in mediocrity. Compare yourself with those who are better placed than you not for competition or envy but as a motivation for you to do better. It will serve to inspire you higher in life. Please ladies lift up your standard. Don't live above your means, just upgrade or update your style as your circumstances get better. Remember, style does not equate expensive. It is time to unleash your unforgettable style.

Principles for Living

- True change comes first with awareness and taking responsibility
- Do not expect others to do for you what you cannot do for yourself
- Do not expect others to invest in you what you cannot invest in yourself
- You must look like where you are going to
- Develop yourself to fit your future
- Dress the way you want to be addressed
- Not taking action is an action itself, same way not making a decision is a decision itself.
- It is not just the things that happened that mar a life; rather it is how people respond to those things that happened.
- The man who fails is not the one who gets knocked down it is the person who can't get back up

Nine

Money is a defence

An Unforgettable Woman has Financial Independence

In the hierarchy of needs physical survival is an essential prerequisite. In today's economies, financial power is reckoned by how much people have physically or potentially because money is now the medium of exchange. If you want to go on a holiday, get food, a good house, electric power supply, heating, anything at all, people require the purchasing power which is money. This goes to show that whoever holds the money has a lot of power in the relationship, they make the decisions, controls and drives situations. Women have traditionally not been seen or used to providing for their homes in the way gender based roles were apportioned. The operative word being that women have not been *seen* to provide . . . What this indicates as we all know very well is that for centuries women have provided for their home in various ways. In Africa, women have been farmers and provided food at harvest time. In the industrial world women were used in production lines and even as soldiers during the war. There have been women leaders, judges, queens and rulers. These activities by women have always been played down and many people send the message to the present day women that she should not be ambitious and be satisfied to be married and play house. Yet no one tells the male populations that they are over ambitious. Now great if that is what the woman wants but if such a decision is imposed by others and it places a woman in a position where she needs to ask another person before she spends even as little as five euros she is in trouble already and suffering in silence or most definitely on her way

Financial control of women as a duty

Relationships where the male partner is the main earner and decides how the family resources are spent sometimes has the potential to place the women back to being dependents. Some of this treatment apportioned to women is tied to a misinterpretation and misunderstanding of many religious, traditional and cultural ideologies. For example, the idea that the man is the head, has been taken literarily to mean that the woman has no head and as such she can't think and cannot be trusted to handle money even when she's the primary earner. We see many women who are impoverished by situations where their spouse or partner collects her pay cheque from her and then administers the 'family funds' **A woman is a person; she has a mind, a will and emotions** as he deems fit. This again puts that woman back in the place of dependency where she has to ask for every penny before she spends it, even when purchasing basic needs such as makeup, a new shirt, tampons or something as small as a fiver for chips. Some people justify this and call it love, some call it trust, others say it is for the self-esteem of their partners and some from religious circles will go so far as calling it submission. Some men actually do this out of a sense of duty, they feel it is their responsibility to lead the home and that for them it usually includes controlling the family funds and dictating how it is spent. Whatever way one looks at it, it is quite disempowering and it can place the woman at risk.

We know that "money is a defense", It is a good thing and it can be a protection in certain circumstances. In fact we know that *a poor person's advice is despised!* Many people misquote and say that money is bad however, if we read the original quotation carefully, it says *"the love of money is the root of all evil,"*. So having money is not a bad thing in fact not having money puts one of the biggest strains on relationship and it also leaves women in a position where they can be easily manipulated.

It can lead to strife, power struggle, abuse, depression, anxiety and constant wrangling's. Research shows that financial dependence on their partners, inadequate resources and lack of options are the main reasons many women remain in abusive relationships.

As women, don't stay stuck, don't limit yourself. Society has changed from the ancient times where women were not openly allowed to work or when married women were asked to stop working or demoted to less public or customer focused jobs. In the financial services in Nigeria a few years ago once their female staff got married the young ladies are moved from customer focused roles where they were account managers canvassing for funds to back office duties. Today you can go as far as you want to in life. It will not be easy as we all know but it is not impossible anymore.

How over protective niceness can lead to financial control

Over protective niceness can be a form of stress in relationships. I don't know about you but I think I am like most women. I will absolutely love the man who asks me to stay at home and do nothing and he pays all my bills and I get to do whatever I want, travel wherever I want to go. Sounds like heaven. So why then do some women who have this lifestyle still complain about it? First we have to see what it cost the woman to be in that position, because dear friend, nothing is free! This usually happens in relationships where one partner stays at home to mind the kids, usually the woman though things are switching around with the economic downturn. This sometimes goes horrible wrong for women for a number of reasons, first instead of giving the stay at home working mum a weekly or monthly allowance which would have been decided by both parties, some men magnanimously gives their spouse a credit card.

Now that sounds great until the bills for the credit card comes and everything the woman has bought is documented and scrutinized. Women in such situations usually feel very constrained though on the surface it seems okay. Its difficulty becomes apparent in the daily practicality when a 45 years old woman has to try and gather all the loose change around the house to get actual spending cash. When everything the woman spends at the end of the month is scrutinised as if she were a child and she has to ask her partner before she can give her child five euros for their school cake sales. So on one hand it seems like a nice gesture and on the other hand it places the woman at the mercy and whim of another human being. A situation which further compounds such women's plight is when the work they do at home is not reckoned as work. She then finds herself in a position where she is expected to be eternally grateful for everything she gets.

The joint account and its potential pitfall

The idea behind having a family fund can be quite good and is even recommended in a healthy, mutually respectful relationship. Women being the way they are very easily take on systems handed down by their parents, group leaders and even their girlfriends without checking to see if it suites their own relationship. Every couple is different and as such your relationship is unique therefore it is vital that people *live with each other according to wisdom*. It is inadvisable for women to consent to every idea proffered by others because not every good idea is necessarily a good one for you. A system that works for others might not automatically work for you so women have to be wise in their decisions. A woman whose partner is addicted to gambling, drugs or even alcohol would need to be careful before having a joint purse with such a person especially if he controls it. If your partner is one given to having extra marital affairs you need to be extra careful if not he will use your salary to womanize, take women on expensive dinners and lavish them with gifts all at your expense.

> *Not every good idea is necessarily a good one for you.*

As good as having a joint purse with your partner can be, it can also be quite challenging first because you will have to rely a great deal on the condition of the heart of the person who controls the purse strings. Some men are great at budgeting and planning and spending on what is important but some are not. So if you have one that is considerate, caring, not power hungry, definitely not a control freak and most definitely not Scrooge then you'll probably be safe. Nonetheless, you have the best awareness about your relationship and partner so trust your inner feelings and instinct. I love the Irish country women's description of a scrooge as a person who can peel an orange in their pocket. If that is your case you will have to explain every single need you have.

Some women have been impoverished especially after their partner's demise even after the years of joint contribution and the years of unpaid work and support where the woman was home taking care of the man and the family while he had the freedom to work and get an education. Many women sacrifice their own education and opportunities for the sake of the family. Extended families have been known to swoop down on the deceased immediate family with women and children sent out of the family home because the family home is in the man's name alone. Don't wait until foreclosure or bankruptcy before you try and put things in your joint names. Families must endeavour to protect each other.

Be wise ladies and do what is best for your home. Make sure it is consciously done and not a system that leaves you and your family at risk of a mountain of unpaid bills. Many women take the position of victim and complain about being maltreated without actually voicing their unmet needs to their spouse or the relevant people such as employers, colleagues, managers, friends and others who are the objects of their frustrations. People are not psychic mind reader so you need to speak up for yourself, really! Ask for what you want, negotiate how you want your home to be, how you want to be treated. *Remember, do not complain about what you permit.* By saying nothing you make such treatment normal and prolonged.

A healthy relationship

Interdependence between a man and a woman in relationship is a healthy form of sharing and it is one of choice. It is one that says "our" not "mine". It promotes team work, it is mutually respecting and beneficial and believes each person is relevant and contributing to the relationship. It is absolutely necessary for the proper functioning of families. If a woman is a dependent in a relationship, a lot of her power to choose is greatly eroded. As unforgettable women begin to negotiate your space because a woman is a person, she has a mind, a will and emotions. She cannot be treated like a slave during the day and expected to perform as a princess at night!

The woman in our story wanted good perfume, she didn't have to beg, steal or borrow to get it. It is good and it feels right for women to have a certain level of independence where she can afford a few comforts for herself, underwear, toiletries, even some food in the house without having to go through twenty questions. A healthy relationship should have mutual accountability which should be consensual and not demanded or taken for granted. The woman should not have to wait till her partner is in good humour before asking for menial things like money for gas, bus fare or food for the home. Such situations can be emotionally trying for women and it has been known to lead to loss of confidence, low self-esteem, bitterness and even deep seated angers from where every evil is borne. In relationships where there are children, the dynamics is usually different and the added pressure or pleasure depending on how people look at parenting affects relationships. It is vital in healthy relationships for the working partner to realize that taking care of the home and kids is not laziness but work. This might help prevent of lot of resentment and feelings of injustice felt by many women. The benefit of this kind of relationship is mutual respect.

> *A woman cannot be treated like a slave during the day and expected to perform as a princess at night!*

For two earners in a family many families have individual accounts and then a third purse to which they both contribute a percentage of their earnings to settle their monthly bills, feeding, rent or mortgage and other joint needs. A system like that provides both parties with financial independence and the safety of having a planned spending for their calculated expenses.

Don't stand still Woman

Having to stay at home for whatever reason is not to be taken as an excuse to let life roll all over her. Life does not have to end. There are ways to remain engaged with life such as online training or distance learning for those who can drag or motivate themselves enough to learn about the computer. There is photography, baking, writing, hair styling, nails or anything at all, an endless list that depends on you, your motivation and expectation of life. It is those who have expectations that get their needs met$_5$. Learn to read or write if you have to or whatever you need or lack because it is never too late to correct a mistake unless left till the person's death.

Women easily blame their partners or having children for not progressing further in life. Some blame it on spouses whom they describe as domineering and not wanting their progress, maybe that is true but you know what, look around you and you'll be amazed how many other women with the same circumstances as yourself are struggling and . . . yes struggling to make it work. Take a look at your neighbour who also has a partner and three children and a career to go with it. Is it easy to manage it all? By no means but as with everything, there is a price to pay and it is usually worth it. We have the choices we make. The life you have today is as a result of the choices you made yesterday. It is not one handed down by life rather it is the fruit of the choices you made yesterday. You can decide to make the kind of choices that will give you the kind of tomorrow you desire in five years from now.

The life you have today is as a result of the choices you made yesterday

Any woman who is not doing something with her life is already treading on dangerous grounds. Women don't habitually live an easy life. It is neither easy for the woman who goes to work and the one who stays at home. However, we can find a way if we really, really, really want it because it's been done before. At a recent Unforgettable Women's Network seminar one female participant at the workshop gave her insight on how she handles her own situation. She said she looks at her life as if she has three full time jobs; the family, full time employment and her Ph.D. programme. It made me think. Sometimes it is just a paradigm shift people need. A switch in the way people look at a situation makes it seem different even when nothing has really changed. Now you have a choice, you can take the easy way out and do the blame game or you can get into the driver's sit of your life and make a change. For an unforgettable woman, the choices you make are absolutely vital. They can make or mar you. The important thing is do not focus on your limitations or what you don't have rather focus on what you have and on your strengths. Educate yourself and improve your skills. You can do it if you really want.

> *Don't focus on*
> *your limitations*
> *or what you*
> *don't have*
> *rather focus on*
> *your strengths*
> *and on what*
> *you have*

Principles for Living

- Apply wisdom to every decision you make as it will help you live successfully with others
- Not every good idea is necessarily a good one for you.
- The people in your life are not psychic mind reader so you need to speak up for yourself.
- Ask for what you want and negotiate how you want to be treated
- Silence can be taken as consent or agreement so speak up
- The way a woman is treated during the day will impact on how she responds at night
- It is those who have expectations that get their needs met,
- A woman is a person; she has a mind, a will and emotions
- The life you have today is as a result of the choices you made yesterday
- Do not focus on your limitations or what you don't have rather focus on what you have and on your strengths.

Ten

Leaving the past behind

An Unforgettable Woman is Not Moved by What People Say

T he world thrives on news so if women can just get it that no matter how an individual is people will always talk. Accepting this simple fact will free a lot of people from heart ache, fear and limitation. What is News? . . . think about it for a minute. It is a compilation of people's stories, mistakes, shame, hurts, good (sometimes), their plans, where and how they live and sometimes who they live with and a whole range of information. Some satellite stations, soft sell magazines, newspapers, and journalists make a living talking about other people. Imagine how boring and uneventful life will be if people could not talk about the things that happened to them. Think of it and how stilted and dull conversations will be if people could not mention things their parents said or did, places they have visited, upsetting incidences or even something as basic as the fall their child had. For some it's talk about the first kiss they were given in high school—that is for those who waited **What people say behind you should be left behind** that long to get it, or just talking about the commotion you witnessed between a couple whom you don't even know! One fact of life is that *people will always talk.*

If you are good, some will like you while others will call you miss goody two shoes, if you are bad, they will call you a 'bad mama' and some might like you just for being bad. It is important to know that whichever way you are people will always talk. One issue that greatly troubles women or maybe I should say one thing that women relationships suffer from is talk. Who said what to whom. The truth is we all do it. Some do it in the guise of care; some say it is concern, some think they are looking for a solution for you. Whatever way you look at it you are sharing information about another person! Now some shared information is not painful for example if someone shares the information that you produce really lovely clothes and directs customers to you that is great and you might even want to say carry on talking. The type of talk that hurts is where the information shared is one you would rather forget about or when the truth is coloured tomake it more sensational. This type of sharing of information is commonly called gossip.

How to handle talk and gossip

Gossip is one of the oldest distribution channels for sharing facts, opinions and even slander or defamations. It wreaks havoc on many female relationships, groups and associations. So it is important that we begin to learn a few skills to handle idle chatter.

1. **Don't share information that is not yours to share**
   The first rule is that whatever you don't want others to do to you do not do it to them! If you start by not being the ones spreading malicious gossip or repeating what people don't want repeated, maybe the world and women groups will be a better place.

2. **Do not participate in gossip**
   Refusing to participate in slander and idle chatter will deter people when they know you will not engage with them. They will stop bringing other peoples issues to you.

3. **Do not speak behind peoples back**

   What you cannot say to people's faces do not say it behind their backs—that is shorthand for gossip.

4. **Gossiping paints you as a gossip**

   Speaking maliciously behind others tells the person you are talking to something about you and that if the occasion arises, you might speak about them in the same way

5. **Remember, what goes around comes around!**

   In other words, what you sow is what you reap. If you cannot take it then don't dish it out.

Looking back

Whatever people say behind your back should be left behind. You have to understand that the minute people talk behind you then that's exactly where they are—behind you. They have admitted that they are less than you, do you understand? They might have more physical possessions than you but the minute they speak behind your back they have upset a principle of life and have positioned themselves behind you. So first you have to be careful as well not to demote yourself by gossiping about others. Everyone has the same twenty four hours so invest yours well. The lyric of an African song in the local pidgin says that *Unforgiveness empowers the past to destroy your future.* "Time na money" meaning time is money, a lovely and meaning song full of advice.

Looking backwards only does one thing, it brings depression. Depression speech is always about what happened! It is always about the past and it portrays someone stuck in the past. Free yourself. Without getting into the whole debate about the medical and nonmedical model of depression the emphasis in this book is that stories associated with depression are always about the past and what happened. Leave them behind if not you bring them into your today and affect your present. People will forget unless you constantly remind yourself by holding it in your mind then you empower the past to destroy your future.

Every time you look back it should be as a learning curve for further reflection and understanding of what could have been done differently and to improve how you handle future similar occurrences.

Looking Forward

What people say in front of you should be left in front and by the time you get there it would have paled and become of no importance. In fact, new information is released at such an astronomical rate that by the time you get to that period or future you are worried about your news will have become old news. So don't worry about it. Many times, people worry what others will say and that in itself is what feeds anxiety. It is good to project and figure out how and what to do when things happen in the future but the fruitless worrying that results in mulling over "what if's" only ends in anxiety and misery. Remember, sufficient unto the day is the evil thereof because tomorrow has enough worries of its own$_2$ As we all know which of us by sitting down and worrying can change even a strand of our hair$_3$ unless of course to make it white or grey! Every time you worry about the future the present passes you by.

Others opinion is not your reality

Now another group of people might be bold enough to look you in the eye and tell you what they really think of you. This one wrecks a lot of women's heads. But I want you to slow down now, go back a few lines and read the sentence again. The operative word there is that it is what *they think* about you. In other words, it is their opinion. What really destroys many women and a person generally is when you take others opinion of you and make it your own. Other people's opinion of you has no power or control over you until you take it and make it your own. The minute you repeat other people's words and

You cannot rise above the level of your thoughts

take their opinions of you as truth it becomes your truth. Know this; you cannot rise above the level of your thoughts. This is one thing a lot of people take for granted and are so unaware of how their thoughts affect their way of being, actions and feelings.

The damage occurs at the point where you take another's persons opinion and so it is no longer their voice you hear in your head, you are no longer just repeating what the other person has told you for many years but this time the voice telling you that you are no good is your own inner voice. Watch out for the place where the inner voice changes from your mothers, fathers, friends, or even teachers to your own voice. That is where the battle is lost. Remember, it is not what goes into a person that defiles him rather it is what comes out of him,. As a rule, I never take other peoples opinion of me as the final word over my life unless of course it aligns with my own opinion. You have to understand that as human beings we are not perfect but are working towards perfection₄. You might not be all that as the American's say but I trust that as you begin to take your power back, you are on the way there.

The Meaning making process and its impact

Many hurts are not really from the words people say rather they originate in the way the words are processed in the mind because people hear, understand and interpret things differently. The way an individual understands a word can empower it and influence its effect. In other words, the meaning associated with words intensifies the pain or produces pleasure. For example, two people are called a piece of paper, one finds it funny and laughs while the other person becomes offended. You know why? It's because one person thinks the words are a silly attempt at insulting her while the other person interprets it to mean she is being seen as worthless. Note that it is her interpretation—even if that was what the person meant. Do you know that other people's words cannot suddenly develop hands and feet, walk into your life and turn you into a piece of paper and neither can it make you worthless. The power truly is in your hands because their words can only transform you to the level you allow it. Unless of course you put hands and feet on the persons words and invite it into your mind where you start mulling over the words to the point you begin to see yourself like that.

The power of your imagination

One of the most impactful principles I have ever come across is the one that says if you can see it, you can have it$_5$. In other words, what you see is what you get. These words ordinarily are promises and principles for you on how to put the power of your imagination to work but many have misused it and have inadvertently allowed it to start working against them. The power of your imagination is just like the law of gravity, the force that pulls all things down. It has been set in motion for the earth to operate effectively and so the imagination has been set to help us as human beings operate effectively. The force of gravity is the reason we are walking on the face of the earth and not floating like helium balloons in the sky.

The fact is that if a human being were to fall down a ten floor story building whether it is a baby, man, granddad or priest they will all splatter on the sidewalk. The reason being that gravity pulls things down. It is important that we understand that the same thing that would work for you if abused or misused can definitely work against you. It does not discriminate or show favouritism at all, not on age, sex, religion or even financial status. Once it has weight, gravity wants to keep it down. In the same way, what you keep seeing long enough will produce. If you keep imagining it happening to you and then you really believe it not the hallucinated belief, then it has a higher chance of actually happening.

You can make your imagination work for you and not against you. Don't act powerless against your thoughts and allow it take you wherever it wants to go. Refute what you don't want, challenge what is not true and think on what you desire$_6$. The human imagination works through thoughts and the thinking process. So to be able to make your imagination work for you, an understanding of how to take control of your thoughts is vital. Thoughts are the little words going around in the mind or should I say inside peoples head. The longer words are allowed to stay in one's mind the stronger they become. Oftentimes people think so deeply, that they produce internal pictures which they can see with their minds eye, this process is called imagination.

Imaginations or the pictures in the head are not there just for fun, they influence actions, further thoughts and feelings. We know that "as a man thinks in his heart so is he"$_7$. In other words, you become what you think, either angry, sad, depressed, lonely, happy, excited, in love even in lust! What you think about long enough you are on your way to becoming and it will certainly influence your actions, it is only a matter of time. It might not be with the person you are thinking but it will happen. The unfortunate thing is that many of us use this very attribute with which we can recreate our world to create and intensify anger, resentment and even fear. The process is that thoughts influence action which influences the human feelings and physiology.

> *You become what you think, either angry, sad, depressed, lonely, happy, excited, in love even in lust*

Thoughts as signals to the body and emotions

Some people wake up feeling depressed. Now what I say especially in Counselling sessions with clients is to get people to go back over the last twenty four hours. The starting point to unravelling the feeling is to locate the trigger. Something usually starts the train of thoughts which in turn affects the person's actions which then goes on to influence the individual's feelings and how they are. It sounds complicated but it is very easy and if you get it you can use it to free yourself and all the shrinks and counsellors will be out of business, at least for a while. Take a few moments now and think about it. For those who wake up feeling depressed in the morning, go back over your thought process from the previous night, who did you talk to and what invitation did you get. One that women easily over look is the movie they saw before going to bed. The romantic fantasy it showed that they have compared with their relationship which has made what she has pale and seem depressing. In fact, some women have described their relationship as a life sentence!

Once you are able to critically retrace your steps in your thoughts process you will unlock the depression, anxiety, fear, loneliness or even feelings of lust. It will help you see why you are suddenly feeling horny or craving a cigarette or a drink. It didn't just come on you suddenly because feelings and cravings are fuelled by thoughts and actions. So mind the thoughts you indulge in. The way it works is that your thoughts influence your actions and your feeling and body responds to their messages and signals. If you go to bed thinking deeply of what is wrong in your life it is not rocket science that you will definitely wake up feeling that *life stinks*. If you don't want that then change the tape you are playing in your head. Change the song you are singing in your head, think on things that are good in your life, think on things that are working, think of what you have rather than what you don't have. Think of what you can do rather than what you can't do.

Feelings and cravings are fuelled by thoughts and actions.

Those who excel is not actually because they are proficient in everything. The secret is just being excellent in one thing and that will place you among the greats of today. But if you go to bed thinking your life is a mess, what happens? . . . you wake up feeling a mess and even more so than you were the day before. It is a simple principle, you think it, do it, feel it and you become it! You think, you do, you feel and you become. I repeated it for emphasis so that you can get it because it is a key to why many people are stuck. The challenge is that it works for good or bad. You think angry you become raging mad and by the time the other person comes back home you have worked yourself up into a right state where you are hopping mad. If you recall the last time you were angry what where you saying over and over in your head, probably, *"I am so mad, I am so mad, I can't believe he said that! I am so mad"* and you ended up very, very mad. Change the scenario and the result will be the same lonely, in love, excited . . . as they say, a word is enough for the wise₁.

It is important to work on your thoughts on a daily basis. For those who don't have major issues yet give it a try from now on. When people say things that are not good or pleasing or commendable refute it and tell yourself that it is just their opinion but I am better than that. Even when thoughts filter into your mind you need to go back in your thinking and take an eraser and rub out those negative, unhealthy thoughts flowing through you and rewrite things in a way that is pleasing to you. You definitely have power and control over your thoughts. The same way you will drive an intruder out of your house, you have to boldly drive away every thought that tries to deprive you of your self-esteem and value. If you leave them even for one minute, it will germinate and grow because thoughts are like seeds₈.

If however the opinion of others is the same as your opinion of yourself then you need to work on that area of your life. If you are willing, you can work out your own change. Don't be among those who sit down and use the children as a cover up for being laidback, refusing to improve themself or learn any skill. *Becoming Unforgettable* is to encourage you to think better of yourself, aspire to greater things, come out of that box and go for your personal best. It is me saying

What you think, you do, you feel and you become

yes you can! Remember your thoughts influence your actions, feelings and outcome in life. To change your present outcome you have to invest in the quality of your thoughts. Who and what is feeding your thoughts. What is your source of information and who are you relying on. In essence, better quality of thoughts will produce better actions which will in turn influence your feeling and the outcome you have.

Important points to note on thinking

- Thoughts are things.
- Thoughts are ideas on wheels
- Your thought cannot be divorced from you
- Human thoughts go everywhere they go
- Thoughts are only as powerful as you allow them to be
- Take an eraser and rub out every contrary thought
- Your thoughts influence your action, feelings and physiology

Don't allow anything steal your life, your joy or your destiny. Remember once more, an unforgettable woman is not moved by what people say. Break free from the control and fear of man, people and things. You have what it takes to win because you were born to win but you have to want it to get it. Life does not give hand-outs on a platter of gold to any one, you have to go to life and take what you want. If you consider oxygen the air we breathe, as free as it is you have to do something for it to become available to you. You have to inhale and exhale. If you don't you will definitely become blue in the face and die! So if you cannot do it yourself and someone or something like a machine has to do it for you then you are again on dangerous territory where you have become dependent. You have to take what you need from life. After all we are humans not robots!

Can Christians use the power of the mind?

I am addressing some Christian doctrines and dogmas because many women are Christian's and they are influenced by their beliefs. As we seek to empower the woman to take her place in the society, her home and community, other relevant issues such as the myths, traditions and customs that might keep women bound need to be addressed.

The first important factor is that there is a difference between the principles of God and the person of God. The principles of God for those of us who believe in the ideology of a creator is that the universe and everything in it is controlled by certain laws that maintain the earthly order. An example will be that when the earth is full of rain it will give its increase$_{10}$, so this helps human beings understand the planting and harvesting seasons. When the sky is full, it gives rain and Scientists came up with what we accept as the water circle. Another law is that whatever goes up must come down and that is the law of gravity. Until of course man due to a need developed something that could defy that law like the airplane. The list is endless but what happens is that such laws are accepted for natural things but when it comes to human beings, people are expected to become like mindless robots and simpletons!

As much as some would love it to be so, there are some laws that operate for everyone irrespective of if you are a Christian or not. Now this baffles many believers but that is what many describe as Mercy. Take for example, when a man and a woman procreate, they produce a child just like themselves, they do not give birth to a cow or a sheep. So there are some principles of God that works in the human body irrespective of whether you are a Christian or not. When the rain falls, it does not select based on whether you are a Christian or not before it chooses to fall on a farm or city. These are all God's principles for the earth and for those who live in it to help the earth function effectively. It is important to note that as a Christian woman you have a mind, a will and an emotion and they all serve a purpose and you can develop and use them to your advantage.

What then is the difference, what is the benefit? Just like the law of aerodynamics which can defy the law of gravity, the person of God uses His God power to make his principles work for a truly believing Christian woman or person faster than it ordinarily would have done. So what you have is a double grace and some call this the supernatural! So for example you can use the power of your mind to create pictures of a desired future but for a believing person, He, God can impute pictures, names people, places and ideas into a willing and desiring mind. It is an awesome place to be for those who really understand it and work at that level of knowing.

Becoming Unforgettable describes the minimum every human being is entitled to as women or men. It documents the principles of the creator but some people can take it a step further and get more out of it because they have access to the person of God.

Principles for living

- People will always talk.
- What people say behind you should be left behind
- Do not live your life based on other people's opinion
- Other people's opinion is only as powerful as you let it be over you
- Peoples opinion of you can only control you to the level to which you allow it
- What you see is what you get.
- What you think about long enough will certainly happen or influence your actions and further thoughts.
- Your imaginations influence your actions, further thoughts, feelings and physiology.
- As you think, you do, you feel and you ultimately become.
- The principles of God are available to everyone but the person of God is only available to believers.
- Whatever you don't want others to do to you do not do it to them[1]
- You cannot rise above the level of your thoughts

Eleven

Living a life of purpose

An Unforgettable Woman has a sense of Purpose

You might have been born physically because a man and a woman came together, however, from before you were born, there was a purpose to your existence. Purpose is the reason a thing exists. Can you imagine that there were over one million sperm cells in the race to fertilise the specific egg from which you were formed. That in itself should influence your self-esteem by first helping you understand that you are unique and you have the makings of a winner. It really doesn't matter what kind of life you have lived until now, the minute you get new truths about yourself you can be empowered by applying such truths to your life. Because it is the truth that you know that makes you free₁. Unless you know why you are alive you will live for others fulfilling their visions and plans for you rather than your own.

Purpose prevents abuse

Though the microphone was made through someone's vision, it however has the unique purpose of amplifying sound so that many people can hear without the presenters and artists bursting their vocal cords. Now if someone doesn't know that it is a microphone or the purpose for which it was made they might just use it to mix flour!

Think about it, if things like microphones, mobile phones all have a purpose then what about you, a woman, a whole person. When people don't have a sense of purpose, they end up going through life doing trial and error. Each individual has a purpose in life and is specially equipped with specific talents for particular tasks.

There is a situation around you now that you have the answer to because you are equipped and on this earth to solve a problem. In other words, you are the answer to the world's problem. The challenge is that women for centuries have been made to feel their purpose was to procreate and serve the male half of the world. The traditions, culture and even various religions have used a male dominated interpretation of principles and doctrines to expound the position and purpose of the woman. If you want to know more watch out for my next book about the female man. It will set you free from human imposed limitations. I imagine that if women were born solely to produce children then they would have been able to do it on their own!

You are not an accident neither are you a product of man's will or lust

Remember an unforgettable woman is a woman of purpose. The big question is what is your purpose in life and why did your parents still produce one more girl after three before you. What is it that those before you were not equipped to do that the earth still needed another female . . . another woman to do. You have to understand that you are not an accident neither are you a product of man's will or lust. You are the solution to a problem on the earth and your value is based on the needs you meet. In other words, the more needs you meet the more valuable you become. So your main job is to first identify the need you were created to meet and secondly, identify what you have in you to meet that need. That is what winners and world changers are made of. The truth is that life will pay you what you are worth. Everyone life has celebrated has been for a specific purpose accomplished. You will not be celebrated for doing nothing or for even planning to do something. It is only the things that you actually do that will count₂.

Discovering your purpose is one thing; doing something about it is another. Dr. David Oyedepo in Nigeria put it succinctly many years ago and it inspired many of us to action. He said "a vision not actioned is

auctioned". Your purpose is the thing you were made
to solve. Remember, everything in life is an answer to
a problem. The need to never miss an important call
has further increased the value of mobile phones
and now we have mobile music and even food on the
go! In life, anything that does not meet a need is cast
away, thrown away and rejected. If you don't want to
be thrown off like some worn out, outdated clothes

***Your
purpose is
the problem
you were
made to
solve***

you need to get cracking with your purpose. A positive factor in all these
is that it is never too late to make the right decision. One of my favourite
sayings is that "only a fool keeps doing the same thing expecting a
different result". So no matter how far gone one is in the wrong direction,
if you keep going that way it is not going to make it right. The day you
get the truth it is your day for change and now is your time. So ladies, get
off that treadmill and go for your gold, your personal best is here.

The minute you stop being able to meet the needs in your partner's
life the relationship goes burst or the cracks begin to show. It is also
the same reason many women are disappointed in love and relationships
because they have learnt to suppress their needs while focusing on
meeting the needs of others then they wake up one day realising they
have mountains of unmet needs. Please do not stagnate in life and end
up being a by word for others. You have to keep improving yourself
because life is dynamic and is constantly changing. Imagine all these time
travel movies if someone who lived one hundred years ago were to truly
be alive today he will almost think the earth has experienced an alien
invasion. Come-on! Think about it, the same clothes you wore ten years
ago you still have that design, the same hair style and perfume —that is
if you use any at all. One is almost tempted to ask what the story is with
some women. It's not even as if they are the most poverty stricken on
the street, just a reflection of their value system. People always somehow
manage to get to spend on what they really need to
spend on. It is always a scale of preference.

If the shoes were reversed and you were your
partner will you fall in love with you? Do you love
yourself . . . do you even like yourself. The rule
is "love your neighbour as you love yourself"₃.
In other words, as you feel, love and care about
yourself, love also the person beside you. Now for

***If you cannot
love yourself
you make
it doubly
difficult for
others to
love you***

many women that is a really tall order because they have been taught this false humility where women are not supposed to look good or see themselves as good or even know how good they are! Remember, if you cannot love you then you make it doubly difficult for others to love you. People perceive the way you feel about yourself and that is usually how they treat you. Anything you can do for yourself is no longer a burden or a pain when you do it for others. It is no longer a big deal and it eliminates the need for ceremonial appreciation.

The way you feel about yourself is obvious from the way you dress, talk, walk and sit. Even the set of your shoulders is also a giveaway sometimes. A strong sense of purpose makes a huge difference in people's life even when the person has not accomplished much it still seems to keep them going. There is a contagious enthusiasm about life when you are around purpose driven people. They plan, set goals and aspire to greater heights, all of which keeps them going and excited about life. It might not be a big gigantic mission like becoming the president of America . . . not that it is impossible if that is your vision. After all who would have said that Barrack Obama would have become the president of the United States of America! Don't be afraid of your dream, don't be afraid to dream. It is the stuff winners are made of. Daring to dream separates those who win from those who don't and it separates those who accomplish from those who don't.

Your dream or purpose might be to raise your children in a certain way, or to work with people with special needs, become a lawyer, writer, or a bus driver. Whatever it is, it has to be something with meaning to you. Remember, it is not the size of your dream that matters it is the need that you meet in others' lives. The reason many people hate Mondays is because they are working in jobs they don't really like. If making a living is the only reason you have that job then it is a bit shallow and it will most likely not bring you real satisfaction. Anytime you *It is not the size of your dream that matters it is the needs you meet in others' lives.* have to give a bit extra to the job, it will be like a huge weight and burden and once Sunday night arrives you start getting stressed. On the other hand, when you work in the place of your purpose, even when it is hard work, you are willing to go on. Even when it is not as financially gratifying as some other things that you could have done, you are willing to hang in there. Having a sense of purpose is what motivates you to go the extra mile at no extra cost.

Diligence is the key to a purpose driven life

Living a purposeful life is exciting, fulfilling and ultimately, rewarding when combined with diligence. A person's gifts, talent, ability or skills will make room for him or her and bring them before greatness₄ but diligence will keep the person there. So your gifts creates opportunities for you but the diligence with which you go after those chances will get you noticed by those who can promote you and increase you. Some believe in luck but pure diligence is more of a sure bet. In other words, you might get the job because you have a great curriculum vitae and your vocabulary in your cover letter is great but if you are not diligent and of good character you will be out of there very quickly!

A purpose driven life as a protection

I am harping on women and abusive relationships because it is more prevalent than is reported. Especially in Africa where I come from it is still so normalized and women are made to feel like "bad women" for resisting or taking action against abuse. People all over the world must take a stand against gender based violence and abuse because every woman irrespective of colour, nationality, education, culture, tradition, religion, immigration or financial status has a right to be safe and respected in her own home. Safety is a right not a choice. Women are made to feel it is okay for another person to be violent to them just because she is female! They are made to feel responsible for the abusers anger . . . they are made to feel responsible for the rapist uncontrollable desires . . . they are made to feel responsible for the unemployed spouse transferred aggression. It has to stop! Like I always say instead of hitting a woman, if a person really wants to fight they should pick on someone their own size and get in the ring. If the rapist likes rough sex he should go to prison and they can rough him up.

Safety is a right not a choice

Don't hang around people who tolerate you, stay with people who celebrate you. Don't hang with people who put you down, or those who constantly highlight your inadequacies, or see you as nothing. Women are manipulated to accept and bear abusive relationships because of what others will say. Really at the end of the day it does not matter what your friends or neighbours think neither does it matter what your mother was able to bear. Remember all the women who did not live to tell their stories and those who have ended up as statistics. Abuse is abuse no matter the reason, age, nationality, culture or religion. I love the Yoruba adage from Nigeria which says "what is not good is not good". In other words, no religion is going to make rape within marriage okay. No reason is going to make financial control okay. No provocation is going to make hitting a woman across her mouth okay. The brutal killing of a Nigerian woman by her husband brought a lot of outcry in Nigeria recently. This woman who had been having marital challenges moved her things and went back to her mother who immediately advised her against it and sent her back to the spouse because she claimed it was culturally wrong and a shame on the family. By the next day this estranged couple had an altercation and he killed her. Another needless life lost . . . another woman who has become a number in statistics.

When the purpose of a thing is not known, abuse they say is inevitable. If your partner does not know your purpose in his life, he might use you as a punching bag and sadly if you don't know your purpose in life you might just let just let them! Many women stay in abusive relationships, they stay there and take it believing it is their cross and lot in life. No woman was made to be abused, raped or brutalized not for war not for fun and definitely not for money. It does not matter your colour, education or financial status, nothing gives any other human being the right to abuse another person and definitely not gender. A purpose driven life will make you detest and resist anything that wants to kill. It will strengthen you against anything that wants to limit you. It will empower you to resist oppression. Don't die ladies because you have a right to live. There is so much the world still

No woman was made to be abused, raped or brutalized not for war not for fun and definitely not for money

needs from you. When I say don't die, it is not only physically women are killed. Some women die a thousand deaths before the real death. There is emotional death, death of friendships, death of dreams, aspirations, desire and even death of women's sensuality. Safety is not a choice it is a right and part of a higher order. Remember, "You must not kill."[5]

Principles for Living

- When the purpose of a thing is unknown abuse is inevitable
- Your purpose is the thing you were made to solve.
- Everything in life is the answer to a problem
- Not loving or valuing yourself makes it doubly difficult for others to love you
- Don't be afraid of your dream, don't be afraid to dream.
- Anything you can do for yourself is no longer a burden when you have to do it for others.
- Your gift creates opportunities for you and gets you noticed but diligence and character will keep you there.
- No woman was made to be abused, raped or brutalized not for war not for fun and definitely not for money

Importance of Purpose

- Your purpose will discipline you
- It will motivate you,
- It releases your creativity
- It will challenge you
- It will propel you forward even when you are weak and feeling discouraged
- It will keep you from being distracted and on track
- It will serve as a target for you and a measuring stick
- It will increase your self-esteem, confidence and it will make you fulfilled.

Twelve

Position! Position!! Position!!!

An Unforgettable Woman is Not Moved by Position

U nderstanding the motive for what people do is very important as it influences actions, expectations, contentment and or dissatisfaction. It makes people's actions either a pleasure or a pressure. Motive is what encourages individuals to take certain action and it makes such actions seem worthwhile. From the story we used at the beginning of this book you will notice that some of the dinner guests wanted to sit on the dignitaries left and some on his right. Some wanted to be his treasurer while some were satisfied just to be his followers. The woman in the story was not interested in getting a position but she simply wanted to do what she felt the timing and customs required. She wanted to meet the need she perceived the dinner guest had. Remember from the previous chapter on purpose, that life will reward you for the needs you meet. This woman's motive was to meet the need of another person, something outside herself while the other dinner guests wanted to meet their own need and that was to gain a position of honour.

Motive influences your Actions

Motive simply put is the reason people do the things they do. If we were to take a trip into your life today what will you say has been the motive for your recent actions? Will it be for love or to meet the needs you have found in others or would it be to please someone making you a people pleaser. Is it by your choice because you really want to or is it forced the one we usually call eye service—just so people can think you are a good person. Many women are so fond of it, they give out presents, designer shirts, perfumes, home cooked dinners and even their hard earned salaries just to impress a fella. No pressure if that's what the woman really wants to do, if however there is an ulterior motive as in that she wants to buy the other persons favour's then she leaves herself wide open for heart ache and hurt. Usually, such ventures don't yield dividends because it is high-risk where you can lose both your capital and investment. Only kidding! . . . There are however very many reasons women make such gestures. Remember as the song writer wrote, "money can't buy you love". In fact no price can be paid for true love. One rule of life that works and reduces heart ache is that *you let your yes be yes and your no be no₁*. In other words, be true to yourself. Pretending never works because the masks always fall off and the cracks will show. Remember your motive impacts your actions so get that motive right.

> *Your motive makes your actions either a pleasure or a pressure*

Recipe for relationship disaster

One reason many women compromise themselves and go into doomed relationships is because of the ticking invisible biological clock. It puts untold pressure on women that this book cannot even begin to document. If at the onset of your relationship you know the relationship isn't going to work, you know you are not attracted to the guy and worse of all you know you will find it hard to submit to his leadership because you don't trust his ability and style of leadership. Going into a relationship like that is a definite recipe for disaster yet so many women do it. After years of marriage some women are frustrated by their relationship because they find themselves tied

> *A union of two incomplete people cannot work as one person will constantly be empty*

within loveless marriages because their motive from the beginning of the relationship was absolutely wrong. If the motive is not love at the beginning, once the initial need is meet and the ulterior motive satisfied all the cracks in the relationship will begin to show. Among the many reasons relationships don't work is because many unions are made up of two needy people looking for another person to complete them. They are looking for people who can meet their needs. So at the end of the day we have a union of two needy and incomplete people. So for some women the motive is to attain the position of wife or Mrs, for others it is the position of mother, some it is just to be some bloke's girlfriend.

The employer—employee relationship can be used as a model to best understand what is lacking in many modern day relationships. Why do you think many employment relationships work? First the employer has a specific need identified and then sets a value for the person who can fill the need. If the employer gets someone worth more than his projection they willingly negotiate and increase his price if the extra resource is available. So two things worthy of note, employers have a job which is a need, secondly they prepare something within themselves to give to the other person—the employee which we call a salary.

The difficulty with many relationships especially from the woman's side is that the motive many times is completely wrong. We have women who want a child because her biological clock is ticking, some is because she is tired of being alone and she needs a bit of company when she comes back from work or she is tired of being the only single person at her friends gatherings, she is tired of answering her parents questions and dodging all the nosy aunties and worse still she is tired of attending every bodies wedding and never her own. The list of wrong reason can fill a book! In fact so many movies have been made about such issues . . . You know what, so many women do it so we will not throw stones. All these motives based on one sided personal needs are great recipes for disaster. What is missing is that many people going into relationships don't bother to do the other half which is to see what they have within themselves to give to the other person in return for getting their needs met. Don't forget, a date is not just to have fun! It is like the interview process in a job selection.

Some men want a gloried big Mama with benefits

If you think women err in one sided needs, you should see the men's list, some have all sorts of request like someone to cook, wash their clothed, pick up after them, clean the house, have their kids and a bit of on demand fumbling in the dark! . . . a litany of requests, an endless list of one sided needs without thinking of what they can give to the other person! Making the woman sound like a gloried big Mama with benefit or perhaps I should say the extra duty of being a bed warmer!

Many women actually try and meet the unspoken list that society has drummed into their subconscious of what a good wife should be and do. What happens is that women decide to be "nice" by giving in to all those demands. They suppress their natural inclination and gut feelings to "submit" to their spouse's demands. The fact is it works sometimes, either short or long term until the guy finds a more willing person to supply his needs. . . . someone needier who is more prepared to offer him much more. If you are married already it is still not too late to try and gently but peacefully renegotiate your space if things are not working. For those who are not married yet then don't throw your life away for someone who mainly wants to take from you because such unions usually ends in misery mostly the woman's. It ends up being an exchange of one set of misery for another.

For all the single ladies

No matter the stories that one might have heard about men, you know the "all men are . . . ." statements, which ends with a string of negative, undesirable traits, well sorry to burst your bubble or disillusion or better still I have hope for you. There are actually still very many men that are not half bad. My younger brother is happily married now so I am not marketing him but I tell you he is a good man. He has the makings of a good man. Look out for a guy that wants you for yourself not for what you can do for him, someone who wants to add to your life and not take away from you.

Love is not sex so don't get bullied by societal thinking

Women need to seriously ask themselves about their motive. For example, the lady having sex with the chap on the very first date is that what you want or do you want to be loved, valued and appreciated. Remember that the date is like an interview process and so if we use that analogy, having sex on the first date is like someone at an interview getting salary advance on a job he has not even gotten not to talk of signed the contract! Call me old fashioned but don't let society bully you with what they call normal into going against your will. Love is more than sex. It can involve sex but it is definitely more than just sex. As my friend Tina would say men give sex for a hug—that is part of their human nature.

Men and women function differently, men are moved by what they see while women are moved by what they hear. The point is if it is just for sex then that is your choice but if you want a serious relationship and your dream is of walking down the aisle, then be careful you have not given all of the main pudding away or allowed too many players to sample or unwrap your gift before the real birthday boy comes. I mean some have tasted so much that by the time they are ready to walk down the aisle they have seen it all with you that they feel the need to go looking for new challenge! Even married women have issues as well when it comes to sexual relations with their spouse and one reason many of them withhold sex from their partners is because it has been reduced to a duty they perform and not an act of love enjoyed between two people as an expression of their feelings for each other.

What kind of man should an Unforgettable Woman Marry?

Any woman who has taken the time to build herself needs to look for a man that allows her to grow. A man who is not intimidated by her future but can allow her live and dream if not he will stifle and suppress that woman. Look for a man you can respect. Not one you hope to respect, not one you pray, wish or hope that you can respect, no one that right now you already respect him. Look for a man you admire not for what he has but for where he could be. He has to be a man of vision. Look for a man you can listen to and allow him lead you. In other words, an unforgettable woman needs to look for a man she trusts his judgment. Very important! For many years I used to say to women look for a man you can live with but I have come to realize that the person you can live with might just as easily be a flat mate. TD Jakes put it concisely when he said "marry the person you cannot live without". I promise you if you only marry him because you can live with him, the day he annoys you too much you will not be willing to make the sacrifice of making it work. Love many say is a choice. If you cannot live without your spouse then it makes the choice of loving them even easier. It means they are not so easily replaceable. However, make sure the feeling is mutual and not one sided if not you leave yourself open to easy manipulation. This type of relationship is not a needy kind of positioning, it is a woman who has a good sense of herself and what she is bringing to the relationship but she is open enough to share it₂.

A date is like the interview process it is not just for fun!

An unforgettable woman needs to make sure her motive is right, not pretended self-sacrificing. When women bear and put up with things they ordinarily would not put up with, when they suppress their needs for the wrong reasons most times than not it backfires. After a few years of continuously living a suppressed life the cracks will definitely begin to show. It is one of the reasons women come away from relationships feeling hurt, broken, used and degraded. Whatever your situation is right now learn from the past, pick up yourself and get building again. As an unforgettable woman don't remain down₃. Whatever you do in a relationship, let it be because you want to as an expression of your love not because you have been forced to do it so you can attain the position of wife, girlfriend or mother.

Misplaced priorities for position

My biggest amazement is that rarely do you find women vying for positions in offices nor do you see many of them get involved in the politics of the corporate world, yet when it comes to contending for the position of a guy's girlfriend or wife, the story changes dramatically. In Ireland there is a big campaign to get more women into politics, how many women are coming out, how many women attend the meetings, how many women have read up on what it takes to develop a political career and campaign. Even with all the free courses, adult education, distance learning and other such initiatives put in place to make education accessible many women are still just satisfied to lay in their own little world watching soaps, home videos and reality shows. Oh and let's not forget those who constantly hold up childcare as a crutch even when their kids have become teenagers already! If the seminar was on how to get a man and keep him I am sure even Croke Park will not be able to contain the attendees! I mean when it comes to relationships, you will see two sisters, cousins, best pals and even a mother and daughter get ready to roll up their sleeves and scratch each other's eyes out. Remember, if you had to scratch out your mothers eyes to get a fella, be careful you won't need to scratch your daughter's eyes to keep him.

If you had to scratch out your mothers eyes to get a fella, be careful you won't need to scratch your daughter's eyes to keep him

There is this ideology our male dominated world has sold to us women and we have swallowed it hook line and sinker without question. Women have been told that there are more women than men in the world, so first they have invoked the idea of scarcity and increased the value of males by drawing on the law of demand and supply. Since women have not questioned it, at a certain age, young ladies and women begin to get that "let the competition begin" feeling. The second idea propagated is that women need to get married and that they need to have relationships, duh! . . . so do men. They have biological clocks as well and many men crave the comfort of a settled home and they definitely long to have their kid not call them granddad! They have all the needs as well as we women do they are just better at hiding it. They don't cry about it or talk about it at every opportunity. News flash sisters, men are just as anxious about settling down as women are.

Some women in desperation are very judgmental and quick to hear sob stories from fellas about their Ex's just because they are seeing themselves as the next Mrs Well I love my African sayings because they are so full of years of tested wisdom. There is one that says "the cane they used to beat the first one is the same one they use on the second wife." So please don't be too quick to judge and step into a relationship with a guy who is bitching about his Ex just because you are desperate for a relationship. Remember whatever you do to get a guy or position you have to keep doing it to maintain it. If you faked being able to work all kinds of computers or you pretended to be able to work very long shifts despite resuming earlier than others you have to keep doing it. If you proved at the start of the relationship that you are miss independent, who pays for her own dinners, carries her own heavy bags, opens her own doors and is in fact supper woman, then please don't complain after five years that he is not doing it. If there is no vacuum, it cannot be filled.

On a final note, let your motive be good and pure. On your own, you might not be able to change this world but you can sure start a ripple effect that will affect your circle of influence. An unforgettable woman is not a selfish self-seeking person, she is not moved by position rather she is moved by a need to add to other peoples lives. The same way the woman's perfume changed the scent of the atmosphere, you too can by your actions of sincerity change your circle of influence.

Principles for Living

- Entering a wrong relationship is an exchange of one set of misery for another.
- An unforgettable woman is not a selfish self-seeking person,
- Whatever you do to get a man or a position you have to keep doing it to maintain it
- Motive impacts on the fulfilment one gets
- Motive influences actions
- Men want a settled home just as much as women, they are just better at hiding it
- Wrong motive will turn you into a gloried big Mama with benefits
- A good relationship is an exchange of strengths and not a union of neediness

Thirteen

The power of a made up mind

An Unforgettable Woman is Decisive

Not knowing what you want as a woman is simply asking for trouble. Life will toss you up and down and give you crumbs if you don't know what you want. Many women go through life ready to take anything and everything and what that does is to reduce life to a game of chance. You cannot play Russian roulette with your life, a game of maybes . . . maybe yes . . . maybe no. If you have not made up your mind what you will or will not tolerate, how far you are willing or unwilling to go and what is too much then sorry to say you will go all the way. A woman who doesn't know what she wants will fall for anything because she has no set boundaries. She has not set her inner parameters and measuring stick that keeps life on course. Sometimes clients say they want any job in my work as a Career Guidance Counsellor I always quickly remind them that such a role doesn't exist. There is no position called "any job".

If you don't know what you want life will give you crumbs

If a woman has not set boundaries about what is acceptable or unacceptable behaviour she will find it really difficult to break out of an abusive relationship. She will keep taking the beating, abuse, even rape in some cases or forced sex for those who don't want to call it rape, until she reaches a point inside herself where everything says enough! Now that point is what is called a made up mind. It is a place of power where a person gets the impetus to make a bold decision. It is the point where people stop wavering between two decisions and they become ready to take the consequences of their actions. You know how it is when a woman is being kicked around either physically or emotionally. Where she is being kicked around and given punches and she cowers in a corner and then more punches are added till she has no more tears? Well most women I have spoken with only do something about their situation when it dawns on them that they or their children could easily be killed that way. That is usually the point where many women snap into action and are willing to take action. Sadly, statistics show that not all women live to tell their story because many women unfortunately leave it too late. Please ladies don't become just a number, do not add to the growing statistics. Nothing, absolutely nothing is worth it.

What happens is that so many women have set the bar very, very low. They only resist abuse when it is almost too late! As it is, we cannot really blame the woman because society has taught her to be very complacent and tolerant of abuse. Worse of it all is that the boundaries have become very blurred between respect, control, submission, religion and duty.

For any woman who has been in an abusive relationship or still is, I cannot profess to know all the facts about your situation, but I encourage you to lift up your standard. Even if you have seen your mother endure years of battery, your friends being beaten and battered by their partners, living in fear and terror of them and sometimes it might seem like the bad guys' always win or goes without punishment. That still does not make it right. Until you as an individual decides that you will not allow yourself be anyone's punching bag, there will be no victory. Where society is now, much of the abuse women experience is within their own homes in their nuclear families. As such, individually every woman has to find her own voice and speak up and hopeful the number of women who get abused will reduce in society, one woman at a time. Then this generation can begin to teach their daughters how to lift up their inner standard, set boundaries and refuse to get abused. These tiny pockets of victories can spread like a ripple effect into your kids and friends lives.

Woman, you are precious and not a punching bag. You are not to be an object for emotional, verbal, physical or financial abuse and control. None of it is allowed. At one time in the world they claimed that people of different skin colour could not sit on the same buses, attend the same schools or play on the same team but all that and more is happening now. So there is hope for the woman that she can be valued in public life and behind closed doors in the secrecy of their homes. Women need to begin to put their minds to work for them. Remember, from previous chapters, you cannot rise above the level of your thoughts. It influences your actions and outcome in life. Who would have thought that before the end of 2010 that we would have an African American as the president of the United States! So there is hope because all things are possible if you believe.

You are precious and not a punching bag

What is the mind?

The mind is the complex of mental faculties that enables us to think, reason, perceive understand and respond to the world around us in an individual way. It is a characteristic of human beings. Simply put, the mind is that part of human beings that collects information, processes it, and then makes decisions. The mind works so fast sometimes people almost thinks that things just happened. That is however not the case because first we receive information which gets processed and it then influences individual actions of act or ignore; fight or flight.

How the mind works

The mind is like the central processing unit of a computer and as we say about the computer, it is "garbage in, garbage out". It works by processing information which it collates from all the knowledge, past experiences, relationships, everything the person knows or is aware of gets rifled through and from similar experiences, the mind makes meaning of new incidences. It also draws from spiritual sources of information such as intuition, premonition and dreams. Based on the interpretation the mind gives to the new occurrence, a decision is reached by the person of how to respond. The mind in essence is the seat of decision, the space where all human data is processed. It is a very important resource that ought to be guarded diligently[2]. It is important that we watch what is allowed in, watch what you allow take residence in your mind because many battles are won and lost there[3] especially in the imagination.

Women have been faced with different norms most of which are unwritten but passed down from generation to generation. They include unspoken rules of how women are expected to behave. They have for years been instructed on how to act, think, be, feel and even what they can aspire to become. They have been coached to believe that some qualities such as boldness, ambition, assertiveness are unbecoming in women. As such, women have formed their identities from such stilted dictates

> **The mind is the seat of decisions where battles are won and lost**

and voices. Because the mind feeds on words and pictures such dictates plays on the mind and begins to mould the person influencing people's beliefs and aspirations. So many women have as a result reached the conclusion that they are no good, they cannot go to school and they cannot learn. The worse is where some women have become resigned and feel there is no need to get educated and some feel there is no need to make an effort. Some are discouraged from getting educated and told that all they need to do is marry a rich man!

Where did you get that idea from, where did your thinking become affected that you feel you cannot succeed in life, where did you learn that as a woman you are nothing! Today you have a choice to make. Either you allow other peoples influence over your mind continue to control you or you take over the reins of your life. Wherever you get the words and pictures that you allow reside in your mind that is what and who controls you. Because ultimately, the information you allow enter into your mind controls your future, what you believe, how you act and who you become. You must understand that your mind belongs to you and it is there to serve you. You are in charge, you are the manager of your mind and you decide who or what allow control your mind[2]. It's time for you to take the reins from your mind before it drives you to destruction. I mean the day your car begins to control you—you are in trouble! It will run you into a ditch but most definitely it will run you off the road. Why then do you think it is okay to let your mind control your life!

The mind does not create new fantasies and it does not tempt people with what they have never seen or heard of. It only entices people with the very fantasies and thoughts they have indulged in. You cannot crave for something you do not know, have never seen or heard about, there's no way. The mind will not be able to comprehend it. Slow down your reading for a few minutes and think about it. Ideas and

> ***Don't let your past destroy your tomorrow, don't drag a disruptive yesterdays into your today***

beliefs come from good and bad experiences with families, parents, siblings, even that uncle who abused you, the boyfriend who jilted you for your best friend. Maybe for someone else it's from the pervert who raped you when you were barely five years old and continued till you were eighteen and strong enough to defend yourself. It is an endless list of nastiness and yes, you cannot undo the past but you can have a better future. Don't let your past destroy your tomorrow, don't drag a disruptive yesterdays into your today. Of course we cannot ignore the media, education system, religion . . . they all impact on what people believe and the ideologies people hold.

Many of us know the story of the woman and the apple. Until that woman saw that the apple was good for food and pleasing to the eyes, nothing happened and she didn't eat it. In such instance, the mind will keep flashing the image of that apple until it is seen as desirable. As human beings, we see, hear and believe things on two levels. One is through the brain which I call head knowledge and the other is through the heart, which is called knowing.

Let your mind work for you

There is a popular saying that there are two types of people in the world, those who make things happen and those who wonder what happened. The woman in our story made up her mind not to let her past failures, mistakes or hurts stop her from getting what she wanted. They were calling her all kinds of names but she had made up her

mind where she wanted to go and she was not prepared to stop short
of the mark. She could have allowed the insults stop her but she didn't.
Remember, it is important not to sweat the small stuff. Focus on your
goal as she did. A double minded man is unstable in all of his ways,
so don't let your mind be swayed back and forth like an unstable reed.
Evaluate and see what you need to accomplish your goal. Women,
learn not to settle for less than your personal best whatever it is. Take
the limits off yourself and go for it whatever your "it" is. It is never
too late to make a change. *An unforgettable woman has a made up mind*
because if you don't know what you want, life will give you crumbs.

Looking like your future

You can make up your mind about the kind life you want. Many
women are quick to wade in with a long list of wants featuring the very
best characteristics. First in the case of relationships, put yourself in
the shoes of the kind of partner you want, if you were him, will you be
attracted to yourself as you are right now. If we carry out a specification
match, you say you want a gentleman, who speaks well, dresses well and
is well groomed, yet you refuse to do that evening course to improve
your diction, you still maintain an ancient hair style, then you are setting
yourself up for heart ache! The question you have to ask yourself is
do you match where you are going? Do you
look like your tomorrow? Success comes when **Success**
opportunity meets with preparation so if you **comes when**
wait till opportunity knocks on your door before **opportunity**
you start preparing then you will already be too **meets with**
late. Are you prepared for your future? Can you **preparation**
attract the kind of future, life, job, career or
relationship you want? It is important from now as an unforgettable
woman to begin to look like the tomorrow you desire for yourself.

One principle in life is for you to look like where you are going.
You have to look the part, talk the part and feel the part. If you say
you want a neat guy who cleans his own dishes and even pulls his chair
back then you cannot be living in a place that is like a dumpster! You
cannot wake up each day on the wrong side of the bed and not be
bothered to wash yourself. Sorry to say, most clean guys will simple

turn around and take off. The woman who wants a man who loves her and then only date guys who spend more time in front of the mirror than herself, eh duh! . . . what do you expect, off course he will love himself more than anyone else. I mean a man who takes longer to get dressed than the woman says something! Another woman claims she wants a motivated bloke and then she dates a man who has not worked for over five years, come-on. Recession or no recession, what happened to flipping burgers even if he claims there are no jobs?

Everything has a price and if you are willing then you can get it$_8$. It is not always a monetary price but it may be the effort you have to make to educate or comport yourself, dress properly and look presentable and real. It is not for you to become a fashion statement but be presentable and represent yourself. Don't forget, you are an unforgettable woman. Strike a balance and try not to swing from one extreme to another. Make your mind work for you not against you. Set your mind on good profitable things. Remember, if you don't stand for something, you will fall for anything.

Principles for Living

- Information is received like signals in the mind, it gets processed and it then influences individuals actions
- The mind is the space where all your data is processed
- You are the manager of your mind and you decide who or what you allow control your mind
- Your mind belongs to you and it is there to serve you
- If you don't stand for something, you will fall for anything
- If you don't know what you want life will give you crumbs
- Indecision is an indication of an absence of boundaries
- Living a life without boundaries is asking for trouble
- The mind is the seat of decisions where battles are won and lost
- The mind feeds on words and pictures

Fourteen

Developing your staying power

An Unforgettable Woman is Persistent

The problem with many people's lives is not the lack of a dream it is the absence of persistent pursuit. Some women give up their dreams and expectations in life when they meet resistance and obstacles. They easily retract and conclude that it was not meant to be especially church folks who become *"super spiritual"*. Do you know that the same way a problem persisted against you and seemed to win, you too can make up your mind that you are going to hold on until your change comes₁. You can decide you won't give up until you get what you want. You can decide to frustrate the problem until it gives up on you. Think about it, instead of me getting frustrated by life and the things that happen to me, I draw on my staying power and frustrate my challenges. If you don't give up you cannot lose.

Failure is not the lack of a dream it is the absence of persistent pursuit.

This dear friend is what is called persistence. To persist means to press on, to keep on, and to continue at a thing. Whatever you do long enough will ultimately produce results. The sad thing is that most of us persist in doing things that are harmful to our health. People persist in harmful habits such as smoking, drinking, pornography, too much TV, shouting, fighting . . . Everyone has the same twenty four hours and the life you have today is based on what you deposit into yours. Some women persist in doing the very things that puts a strain on their relationship. That kind of persistence will ultimately lead you to a break up and send you down to the divorce courts.

Persistence does not mean being obstinate or blind to reason. It simply means being creative enough to change your methods. If you have tried a particular method and it doesn't seem to be working then change something, try something different. It might not be what you are doing that is not working but *how* you are

> ***The life you have today is based on what you do with your twenty four hours.***

doing it. Don't be discouraged, don't run away, don't give up and don't hide away from the society change your method!

One of the most important questions you can learn to ask yourself when you are faced with a challenge is the question *how*. It is a great question that commands an answer. It actually draws an answer like an automatic response. I encourage you to mull over that question concerning any issue you are having and in a very short time you will be amazed at how many ideas and suggestions you will get. For example the person who wants to work but has two children and the recession makes it really hard to find work and you have the added problem of childcare. You just start asking that question to yourself and to people around you who you respect within a week you'll be amazed at the wealth of information and resources just around you that you have not been taping from. Remember information is a key to success.

The woman in our story was jittery walking through a room full of men talking down at her yet she didn't stop. Remember failure is not a person, it is an event and you have not failed until you stop. Irrespective of what people say if you really believe it and you really want it, then go for it₂. If you can dare to dream it then hold on to that dream because you can have it. No matter how impossible the dream might seem, just dare. The Wright brothers dared in the face of impossibilities and they put a plane in the sky. People laughed at them, said it was not possible but today there is a metal bird in the sky that can carry people from one place to the other. This metal contraption is what we all call the airplane. Don't forget it was someone's dream. Everything you are enjoying today and even taking for granted was all an idea, a dream in someone's mind that persisted in the face of doubt, challenges and all kinds of obstacles. They are ideas that persisted in the face of many failed attempts. Remember you have not failed until you stop.

Mount Everest is a place full of people's dreams where some fell along the way but persistence took many all the way to the very top. Press on dear woman, don't give up, don't allow yourself to be bullied, don't allow anyone tell you what you can and cannot do. Do not allow circumstances dictate to you. Persist because you are destined for greatness. No matter where you are now you can make it. It is never too late. Don't believe that lie that most women spin to themselves and to each other, "it is too late for me now, my time has passed, I have missed my season". *Who told you that?* You can decide which report you want to believe that it is too late or that there is still a chance for you to make something of your life. Take that chance no matter how small it seems. Most good things start small. Remember even a journey of a thousand miles begins with what? . . . the first step! Unless you take that first step nothing will happen. Please take that step, make the move and do it now. Many unforgettable moments awaits you!

Principles for living

- Failure is marked not by the lack of a dream but the absence of persistent pursuit.
- Persistence is not synonymous with being obstinate
- Don't change the dream, change the method
- The question how is one question that commands an answer
- You have not failed until you stop
- Failure is not who you are, it is an event that happened.
- Everything you are enjoying today started as an idea and a dream in someone's mind
- Most good things start small

Fifteen

Let's talk about Submission

An Unforgettable Woman Knows Who to Submit to

The subject of submission is very serious and delicate because it holds the key to a peaceful coexistence between the male and female populations of society. The concept takes its origin in many strong religious, cultural and traditional doctrinal teachings and ideologies which are still being handed down through the years. The subtleness required in addressing the issue of submission is mainly because the aim is not to stir up strife or resentment between males and females in intimate relationship but to restore the original intention and purpose to the order of their dealings. It is sad to say though that the subjugated treatment of women is not limited to families but is prevalent even in public life and women have over the years come out the worse while the male population have had the privileges out of both sexes.

Female subjection in the name of submission has been used by some as a license to abuse, control and demean women. It has resulted in many of the attributes associated with adulthood being stripped away from them. For example, the right to make their own decisions, financial independence, equal treatment and opportunities, respect, and autonomy. Such mistreatment is mainly due to a lack of proper understanding of the purpose and value of the woman. As we very well know, when the purpose of a thing is unknown, abuse is inevitable particularly where women issues are concerned. Some people have erroneously seen the woman as an object of male pleasure while some see her as a care taker. Other roles she has been assigned include personal slave, child bearer, cleaner and of course driver. In fact some people expect the woman to be a beautiful princess in public, a glorified big mama in the house and a tigress in bed!

Though such positioning of women is more prevalent in some countries and communities than others, it is not limited to them. In nations the world over, we see that women earn less than men in similar roles. We see the glass ceiling where the upper management levels have fewer women even when studies show that there are more women with educational qualifications now than men in some countries. *Submission is not a license to abuse, control and demean women* We see that women are automatically expected to be the ones to stay at home and care for the children. We see that women do a full day's job at their paid employment outside the home and most of them are still expected to be the main home caretakers after long hours at work. Some people will find it unbelievable and even strange but in some African homes even in the diaspora, the woman is expected to kneel down when serving a meal to her spouse! What I don't understand is how the person who loves and sleeps with a woman allows her do that and doesn't stop such obeisance from one human being to another. In some other relationships, women are not expected to question anything their partners say nor are they expected or even allowed to have a different idea and opinion.

This subjugation of women is the one practice where religious groups who never agree with each other actually agree. Cultures that abhor each other and are at logger heads all agree on the idea. In fact traditions and rulers that have contrary belief systems where some believe that one is decadent and the other is barbaric all agree on the subservient positioning of the woman. Amazingly, some women who have developed personally in leadership, older women, mothers who have experienced this and seen the ills and effects on women are used to perpetuate and enforce this ideology. It is bandied about all over the world even in societies where there seems a less obvious disparity between men and women in public life. It still operates covertly and within the home in familiar relationships.

125

To Love or to Rule

We know that a wise woman builds her home while a foolish woman pulls hers down[1]. However, a lot of the interpretations and messages that has been handed down for centuries have come from a male dominated understanding. As a society, we suffer from male supremacy in the exegesis of the word, understanding of policies and ideas. This concept of submission has by a male led interpretation been expounded to mean doing whatever the woman's partner asks for even if it means her acting like a mindless simpleton with no care for her body and health.

The woman in the story from which these twelve qualities of an unforgettable woman were extracted was in a room full of men where anyone of them could very easily have been her partner. All the men who were at the same human level as her only saw one thing. They did not see who she could be, they did not see where she could go neither did they see what she could become. They focused on her past and her apparent present. They imagined her future and found her wanting; they found her unworthy and desired her to be quiet and hidden away with no prospects. They tried to limit her dreams and vision yet it didn't stop her. They called her undesirable names and underestimated her potentials. In summary they boxed her up and relegated her to obscurity. Sadly, that is the level many women have been placed today in their homes and society where many are suffering in silence. Many women have resorted to living a double life where on the outside they look very happy as if they have no care in the world yet on the inside they are irritable, full of bitterness, pain, hurt, shame and anger due to a sense of injustice. As troubling as this is, women often feel very underequipped to handle it and very few actually do mainly because they feel there is nothing that can be done and some believe it is their lot in life. Some people go so far as to believe it is how women are supposed to be treated.

> **The woman is expected to be a beautiful princess in public, a glorified big mama at home and a tigress in bed!**

In the family system various orders have been put in place to help it run smoothly. One of the ones I am conversant with first instructs people in relationships to submit to each other[2]. Many people miss this and go straight to the

second part which says wives should submit to their spouse₃. This is one
of the main root causes of a lot of strife in homes because of the way it is
practiced. It disables the woman's autonomous self and disempowers her.
The beautiful thing is that the woman in our story did not pay attention
to the others at that meeting because they were not her connection.
Thankfully there was another guest in the room who while the others
were stuck in her past and her limitations he saw her potential. That is
love, the kind that doesn't think cruelly of the other₄.

The first set of liberating facts for women is that an unforgettable
woman knows who to submit to, when to submit and most importantly
she submits to love. Please Sisters, this time I call you sisters, whether black,
white, red, green, pink or blue. We have been called to have proper order
in our home and the call is that women should submit to their partners
who are to love them. However, for it to be a productive relationship, they
must first submit to each other. In other words, they are to be considerate
and value each other as they value themselves₉:₄. This submission is to
love not force and love and force are never interchangeable. While the
woman in our story was still undesirable and underserving the dinner
guest loved, valued and called her commendable. Ladies, you have
been asked to submit to what brings out the best in you! That is love.
Unfortunately, force does not work though it is often used by males to
forcefully gain control of their relationship. Ultimately it doesn't work
neither does, bullying, name calling, embarrassing... none of them works.
Rather, it breeds resentment and you find that relationships and societies
with more inequality in treatment between males and females are more
backward, less developed and welcoming. They have fewer truly happy
relationships which with time becomes more of a duty characterised by
doing rather love based which is characterised by being.

Women have been called to submit to a loving person who can still
love you in spite of. You are called to be loved, esteemed and protected,
think about it, how does hitting a woman across her pregnant tummy
equal protection, how does that equal love.

Fearful Submission

We know very well that the effect of force is short term if not the
prisons would be empty by now as the world would have been crime

free. In fact the States where they still have the death penalty system should be absolutely crime free now. You know what . . . it isn't because force doesn't work. Love is the key to unlock an unforgettable woman. In considering the way women are treated in relationships by their partners, it is important we refer to the some of the sources of such ideas. One view says the man should treat his partner as he would his own body$_5$. The understanding of this command seems completely ignored in society or otherwise it is lost. It is however one of those rules set in place to help human beings show consideration and value for each other because in intimate relationships, the human conscience is the law and many people have muted its voice.

A woman is supposed to be treated by her partner the same way he treats his own body exhibiting the same level of care and understanding$_5$. So if you see a man using his two fist to pound at his chest and tummy what picture does that paint? Demonstrate it and see . . . exactly! Well that is what is happening every day to some women. Also, imagine a man looking at his right wrist and slamming it on the table, he begins to curse at his hand with all obscenities. What will you say? Again, that is what it is like when a man verbally abuses his spouse. Some people skip those commands that encourage mutual consideration and care and go straight for the ones that serve their purpose. Another part of that same text says *do not defraud one another$_6$*.

Many men love this one as they have literarily taken it to mean sex on demand! Again if the woman is to be treated as the man's body then forcing a woman to have sex as a marital duty can be likened to the man forcing his own body. It is like a man ignoring the *Submit to love because love and force are never interchangeable* tiredness of his body or his emotional state and pressuring his body by trying every hand trick to force a sexual response from his body! The thing is people want the benefits without the responsibility. Though you have to be careful that you are not withholding sex from your partner as a weapon, punishment or bargaining chip. That will be bothering on unfair play!

This need for control also plays out in families in transferred aggression from one person to the other. Many homes today are wracked with hostility because the husband who is the head of the home uses force to get the kind of behaviour he wants from his wife and then the woman uses force to get the children to behave the way she wants them to. These kids join the spiral of aggression by using force on each other and this very easily can be seen culminating in playground violence in school! The kid gets in trouble and the aggression intensifies and starts again between the parents. So many homes have ended up being a zone of anger and aggression. This has short changed so many people because it does not create the loving and nurturing environment people crave going into relationships neither does it create the haven and rest marriage is supposed to be. Marriage is a beautiful union of two people who are ready to experience life on a different level. Society and individuals have to get back to the original way it was meant to be.

At conferences you hear women who have taken the subject of submission to all new levels. Some ladies know their partner is sleeping around with other women and that he is having unprotected sex with them which they know for a fact seeing he has had two children outside their matrimony with these other women. Many women are uncertain how to respond in such situations not because they think it is right . . . not because they are not hurt and upset . . . but because they believe that submission expects them to do nothing! They feel they have to continue having unprotected sex with a cheating promiscuous spouse even in the face of HIV Aids and all manners of sexually transmitted diseases because of their belief, their understanding of submission and pressure from outside sources including parents, friends, group leaders and what others will say. Another rule from the same source says "if you join yourself with another person sexually you become one body with them[7]". So how many people should women have in their marriage bed? How many is too much. Unfortunately in marriage and consenting relationship, the two individuals involved are responsible for their actions and behaviour. As creatures of choice you have the responsibility for what you accept.

Three is a crowd in the marriage bed

Some women find themselves caught in a dilemma of doing what is right for themselves or what others say is right. For example a woman who knows her partner is a gambler or spendthrift and still gives her salary and child benefit payments to such a man will need to decide for herself if that is submission or being unwise! Remember, a wise woman builds her home$_1$. What is your interpretation of a wise woman and what will you expect her to do? At the end of the day what happens with many homes is the woman ends up not being able to pay the children's school fees, they end up wearing torn clothes to school. They can't afford for them to go on school trips with their mates and many women become very inventive about why the tooth fairy and Santa Clause always misses their house! Ultimately women and children suffer because their lives are jeopardized and put at risk of poverty. You have to decide what is wise for your home, it is an individual responsibility. Many women have saved their children and household by holding on to the truth$_8$. You can too because a lot of behaviours women call submission is a reflection of personal fears.

The woman in our story submitted to love, please read the story. If she submitted to bullying or intimidation she would not have made it through the door in the first place and definitely not into the room. Her destiny would have been closed off. Remember, women are responsive beings who are drawn to love. Any man who wants the best of a good woman or an unforgettable woman must first learn how to love her the way she ought to be loved.

Conclusion

The quality of our society cannot be better than the quality of life of its women folk because there is always a woman in the life of every man. If you change a woman you change a whole family, community and society. This woman can be a mother, a sister, wife, girlfriend, boss, secretary, teacher or any woman at all because every woman is important. Their reach makes them a vital part in the transformation of society. However, people can only give out of what they have. That is why it is vital that we all work together to create the situation in which women are happiest and most effective. Not just for public display but in the privacy of her home, private offices and groups. The whole society has the combined responsibility to help the woman be her best. When you support a woman's development you are ultimately helping yourself so all of society must understand that we have a vested interest in supporting the woman in discovering and walking in her full element.

Becoming Unforgettable is an extract of the intrinsic and indispensable properties that serve to characterize and identify the woman as she was meant to be. They are the crucial elements that will bring the woman ultimate fulfilment and help her find her place as it was meant to be and not how or where others have decided for her.

Becoming Unforgettable through the insightful analysis of the life an everyday woman highlights twelve qualities that will bring about change by recognising and releasing the essence of the woman. The underpinning principles show that the power truly is in your hands. Ladies, it is time to take the reins and get into the drivers sit of your life. Don't wait for anyone to do it for you. Don't wait for people to affirm you. As you embark on this journey of transformation your unforgettable moments will establish you and bring your true fulfilment because you are destined for greatness. Remember your greatness is not reckoned by what you have rather it is weighed by who you are. Don't let anything or anyone take your strength. Your best days are here as you engage with these time tested principles which are capable of break barriers and transforming the life of every woman who is ready for her change.

Not everything in this book is going to be for you, so take what you need and leave the rest. It has encouragement for those who are dissatisfied with where they are and with the results they have got so far. It gives women options that will enable them make more informed decisions. It has hope for the woman who is feeling disempowered. My hope is that women who are tired of their present position and are looking for change will find something in this book that will lead them to live a more fulfilled life.

Becoming Unforgettable is a book written from a heart encouraging you to think better of yourself, aspire to greater things, come out of every human inflicted limitation and go for your personal best. There are three possible choices you can make, up, down or stagnate; left, right or stand still; positive, negative or neutral. I truly trust that you will make the best decision and become the Unforgettable Woman you were born to be.

I will be delighted to hear from you. So please feel free to contact me and leave your comments, responses or any unanswered questions you have been left with.

Summary

12 QUALITIES OF AN UNFORGETTABLE WOMAN

An Unforgettable Woman Is Bold
An Unforgettable Woman Takes the Initiative
An Unforgettable Woman is Knowledgeable
An Unforgettable Woman is Caring and Tender
An Unforgettable Woman is Stylish
An Unforgettable Woman has Financial Independence
An Unforgettable Woman is Not Moved by What People say
An Unforgettable Woman has a sense of Purpose
An Unforgettable Woman is Not Moved by Position
An Unforgettable Woman is Decisive
An Unforgettable Woman is Persistent
An Unforgettable Woman Knows Who to Submit to

Contact

To schedule a seminar, workshop or group facilitation session with your group, or to order Ebun Akpoveta's tapes and books please contact

Tel: 00353 89 418 5169, 00353 87 131 11402
Email: unforgettablewoman.eb@gmail.com
ebunveta@eircom.net
www.tuwn.org
http://www.facebook.com/TUWNIreland
http://www.facebook.com/BECOMINGunforgettable

To attend one of the Unforgettable Women's Network Monthly Seminar you can find us on Facebook to get updates of our meeting dates. We run a three hours session on the 2nd Saturday of every month from 2-5pm The Unforgettable Women's Network is a Women's organisation with a vision to transform society, one woman at a time using time tested principles to develop lives.

Notes and References Guide

Chapter Two

1. **Matthew 26: 8**—When the disciples saw this, they were indignant. "Why this waste?" they asked.

2. Mark 14:3—While he was in Bethany, reclining at the table in the home of a man known as Simon the Leper, a woman came with an alabaster jar of very expensive perfume, made of pure nard. She broke the jar and poured the perfume on his head.

3. **Luke 7:37**—When a woman who had lived a sinful life in that town learned that Jesus was eating at the Pharisee's house, she brought an alabaster jar of perfume,

Chapter Four—Bold and Beautiful

1. Mark 7-**7** Howbeit in vain do they worship me, teaching *for* doctrines the commandments of men. 8: For laying aside the commandment of God, ye hold the tradition of men, *as* the washing of pots and cups: and many other such like things ye do. **9:** And he said unto them, Full well ye reject the commandment of God, that ye may keep your own tradition.

2. 1ˢᵗ John 4:18—There is no fear in love; but perfect love casts out fear: because fear hath torment. He that feareth is not made perfect in love

3. Philippians 4:8—Finally, brethren, whatsoever things are true, whatsoever things *are* honest, whatsoever things *are* just, whatsoever things *are* pure, whatsoever things *are* lovely, whatsoever things *are* of good report; if *there be* any virtue, and if *there be* any praise, think on these things.

4. John 8:32—And ye shall know the truth, and the truth shall make you free.

5. proverbs 23:7ᵃ—For as he thinketh in his heart, so *is* he:

6. John 19:30—When Jesus therefore had received the vinegar, he said, It is finished: and he bowed his head, and gave up the ghost.

7. psalm 118:17—I shall not die, but live, and declare the works of the LORD

8. Mk 11: 23 For verily I say unto you, That whosoever shall say unto this mountain, Be thou removed, and be thou cast into the sea; and shall not doubt in his heart, but shall believe that those things which he saith shall come to pass; he shall have whatsoever he saith.

9. Psalm 11:3 If the foundations be destroyed, what can the righteous do?

10. Mark 12:31 And the second *is* like, *namely* this, Thou shalt love thy neighbour as thyself

11. Proverbs 5:—15 Drink waters out of thine own cistern, and running waters out of thine own well, **16** Let thy fountains be dispersed abroad, *and* rivers of waters in the streets. **17**Let them be only thine own, and not strangers' with thee. **18** Let thy fountain be blessed: and rejoice with the wife of thy youth. **19***Let her be as* the loving hind and pleasant roe; let her breasts satisfy thee at all times; and be thou ravished always with her love. **20**And why wilt thou, my son, be ravished with a strange woman, and embrace the bosom of a stranger? **21**For the ways of man *are* before the eyes of the LORD, and he pondered all his goings.

Chapter Five—Spicing Up Your Life

1. James 1:22 But whoso looks into the perfect law of liberty, and continued *therein*, he being not a forgetful hearer, but a doer of the work, this man shall be blessed in his deed

2. Ecclesiastes 7: 12 For wisdom *is* a defence, *and* money *is* a defence: but the excellency of knowledge *is, that* wisdom gives life to them that have it

3. 1st Timothy 6:10 For the love of money is the root of all evil: which while some coveted after, they have erred from the faith, and pierced themselves through with many sorrows.

4. Psalm 75:6: For promotion *cometh* neither from the east, nor from the west, nor from the south. 7: But God *is* the judge: he puts down one, and set up another

Chapter Six—Knowledge Opens Doors

1. Proverbs 4:7—Wisdom *is* the principal thing; *therefore* get wisdom: and with all thy getting get understanding.

2. Proverbs 24-**3** Through wisdom is an house builded; and by understanding it is established: **4** And by knowledge shall the chambers be filled with all precious and pleasant riches. **5** A wise man *is* strong; yea, a man of knowledge increases strength

3. Hosea 4:6ª—My people are destroyed for lack of knowledge: because thou hast rejected knowledge, I will also reject thee,

4. John 8:32—Then you will know the truth, and the truth will set you free."

Chapter Seven—You Don't have to be a Boy to Make it

1. Proverbs 14:1—The wise woman builds her house, but with her own hands the foolish one tears hers down.

2. 1st Peter 3:3a—Your beauty should . . . 4 Instead, it should be that of your inner self, the unfading beauty of a gentle and quiet spirit, which is of great worth in God's sight.

Chapter Eight—Modest but Stylish

1. James 5-**13** Is any one of you in trouble? He should pray. Is anyone happy? Let him sing songs of praise. **14** Is any one of you sick? He should call the elders of the church to pray over him and anoint him with oil in the name of the Lord. **15** And the prayer offered in faith will make the sick person well; the Lord will raise him up. If he has sinned, he will be forgiven. **16** Therefore confess your sins to each other and pray for each other so that you may be healed. The prayer of a righteous man is powerful and effective.

Chapter Nine—Money is a Defense

1. Ecclesiastes 7:12—For wisdom *is* a defense, *and* money *is* a defense: but the excellency of knowledge *is, that* wisdom gives life to them that have it.

2. 1st Timothy 6:10—For the love of money is a root of all kinds of evil. Some people, eager for money, have wandered from the faith and pierced themselves with many grief's.

3. Ecclesiastes 9:15-16—Now there lived in that city a man poor but wise, and he saved the city by his wisdom. But nobody remembered that poor man. **16** So I said, "Wisdom is better than strength." But the poor man's wisdom is despised, and his words are no longer heeded.

4. 1st Peter 3: 7—Likewise, ye husbands, dwell with *them* according to knowledge, giving honour unto the wife, as unto the weaker vessel, and as being heirs together of the

grace of life; that your prayers be not hindered. **8** Finally, *be ye* all of one mind, having compassion one of another, love as brethren, *be* pitiful, *be* courteous:

5.   live with each other according to wisdom

6.   Proverbs 23:18—For surely there is an end; and thine expectation shall not be cut off.

Chapter Ten Leaving The Past Behind

1.   Mark 7:17-**15** Nothing outside a man can make him 'unclean' by going into him. Rather, it is what comes out of a man that makes him 'unclean

2.   Mathew 6: 34—Therefore do not worry about tomorrow, for tomorrow will worry about itself. Each day has enough trouble of its own

3.   Luke 12: **25**—Who of you by worrying can add a single hour to his life **26** Since you cannot do this very little thing, why do you worry about the rest?

4.   Genesis 11: 6^b—And the LORD said, Behold, the people *is* one, and they have all one language; and this they begin to do: and now nothing will be restrained from them, which they have imagined to do.

5.   Genesis 13:—14 And the LORD said unto Abram, after that Lot was separated from him, Lift up now thine eyes, and look from the place where thou art northward, and southward, and eastward, and westward: **15** For all the land which thou seest, to thee will I give it, and to thy seed forever.

6.   Mathew 11: 12—And from the days of John the Baptist until now the kingdom of heaven suffereth violence, and the violent take it by force.

7.   Philippians 4:8—Finally, brothers, whatever is true, whatever is noble, whatever is right, whatever is pure, whatever is lovely, whatever is admirable—if anything is excellent or praiseworthy—think about such things

8.   Proverbs 23:7^a—For as he thinks in his heart, so *is* he:

9.   Mark 4:14—The sower sows the word.

Chapter Eleven Living a Life of Purpose

1.   John 8: 32—And ye shall know the truth, and the truth shall make you free.

2.   Romans 2:13 (For not the hearers of the law *are* just before God, but the doers of the law shall be justified.

3.   Mark 12:31 The second is this: 'Love your neighbour as yourself.' There is no commandment greater than these."

4.   Proverbs 18: 6 A man's gift makes room for him, and brings him before great men

5.   Exodus 20:13—Thou shalt not kill

6.   Proverbs 22:29—Seest thou a man diligent in his business? he shall stand before kings; he shall not stand before mean *men*.

Chapter Twelve Position, Position, Position

1.   Genesis 2:25—And they were both naked, the man and his wife, and were not ashamed.

2.   James 5:12—Above all, my brothers, do not swear—not by heaven or by earth or by anything else. Let your "Yes" be yes, and your "No," no, or you will be condemned.

3.   Proverbs 24: 16 for though a righteous man falls seven times, he rises again, but the wicked are brought down by calamity.

4.   Psalm 34: 19—A righteous man may have many troubles, but the LORD delivers him from them all;

Chapter Thirteen—The power of a made up mind

1.   Philippians 4: 7—And the peace of God, which transcends all understanding, will guard your hearts and your minds in Christ Jesus. 8. Finally, brothers, whatever is true, whatever is noble, whatever is right, whatever is pure, whatever is lovely, whatever is admirable—if anything is excellent or praiseworthy—think about such things. 9. Whatever you have learned or received or heard from me, or seen in me—put it into practice. And the God of peace will be with you.

2.   Proverbs 4: 23—Keep thy heart with all diligence; for out of it *are* the issues of life.

3.   2nd Corinthian 10: 4-5—(For the weapons of our warfare *are* not carnal, but mighty through God to the pulling down of strong holds;) 5 Casting down imaginations, and every high thing that exalts itself against the knowledge of God, and bringing into captivity every thought to the obedience of Christ;

4.   Romans 1: 21—For although they knew God, they neither glorified him as God nor gave thanks to him, but their thinking became futile and their foolish hearts were darkened.

5.   Genesis 3:6 And when the woman saw that the tree *was* good for food, and that it *was* pleasant to the eyes, and a tree to be desired to make *one* wise, she took of the fruit thereof, and did eat, and gave also unto her husband with her; and he did eat

6.   Mark 11:23 For verily I say unto you, That whosoever shall say unto this mountain, Be thou removed, and be thou cast into the sea; and shall not doubt in his heart, but shall

believe that those things which he saith shall come to pass; he shall have whatsoever he saith

7.   James 1:8 A double minded man *is* unstable in all his ways

Chapter Fourteen—Developing Your Staying Power

1.   Romans 4:18 Who against hope believed in hope,
2.   Mark 11:23 For verily I say unto you, That whosoever shall say unto this mountain, Be thou removed, and be thou cast into the sea; and shall not doubt in his heart, but shall believe that those things which he saith shall come to pass; he shall have whatsoever he saith

Chapter 15—Let's talk about Submission

1   Proverbs 14:1 Every wise woman builds her house: but the foolish plucks it down with her hands
2.   Ephesians 5: 21—Submitting yourselves one to another in the fear of God.
3.   Ephesians 5: 22—Wives, submit yourselves unto your own husbands, as unto the Lord. **23** For the husband is the head of the wife, even as Christ is the head of the church: and he is the saviour of the body. **24** Therefore as the church is subject unto Christ, so *let* the wives *be* to their own husbands in everything. **25** Husbands, love your wives, even as Christ also loved the church, and gave himself for it; **26** That he might sanctify and cleanse it with the washing of water by the word, **27** That he might present it to himself a glorious church, not having spot, or wrinkle, or any such thing; but that it should be holy and without blemish.
4.   1ˢᵗ Corinthians 13:—**4** Love is patient, love is kind. It does not envy, it does not boast, it is not proud. **5** It is not rude, it is not self-seeking, it is not easily angered, it keeps no record of wrongs. **6** Love does not delight in evil but rejoices with the truth. **7** It always protects, always trusts, always hopes, always perseveres. **8** Love never fails.
5.   Ephesians 5: 28 So ought men to love their wives as their own bodies. He that loves his wife loves himself. **29** For no man ever yet hated his own flesh; but nourishes and cherishes it, even as the Lord the church: Treat her like your own body **28** So ought men to love their wives as their own bodies. He that loves his wife loves himself. **29** For no man ever yet hated his own flesh; but nourishes and cherishes it,
6.   31ᵇ . . . and they two shall be one flesh. 33 Nevertheless let every one of you in particular so love his wife even as himself; and the wife *see* that she reverence *her* husband.

7. Mark 10: 8—and the two will become one flesh. So they are no longer two, but one.

8. 1ˢᵗ Samuel 5: 25-**32** David said to Abigail, "Praise be to the Lord, the God of Israel, who has sent you today to meet me. **33**May you be blessed for your good judgment and for keeping me from bloodshed this day and from avenging myself with my own hands. **34** Otherwise, as surely as the Lord, the God of Israel, lives, who has kept me from harming you, if you had not come quickly to meet me, not one male belonging to Nabal would have been left alive by daybreak." **35**Then David accepted from her hand what she had brought him and said, "Go home in peace. I have heard your words and granted your request."

9. 1ˢᵗ Corinthians 6:—**16** Do you not know that he who unites himself with a prostitute is one with her in body? For it is said, "The two will become one flesh."

Lightning Source UK Ltd.
Milton Keynes UK
UKOW030043031012

199926UK00002B/10/P

9 781477 226261